The Trumpeter's Handbook

Roger Sherman

The author holds the Bachelor and Master of Music degrees in Music Education and the Performer's Certificate in Trumpet from the Eastman School of Music. He has studied trumpet with Edwin Betts, Sidney Mear, Armando Ghitalla, Bernard Adelstein, and Charles Hois.

At present he is a member of the trumpet section of the Pittsburgh Symphony Orchestra and adjunct faculty member at West Virginia University. Mr. Sherman has previously been first trumpet with the West Virginia Symphonette and the National Ballet of Canada, Assistant Chairman of the Division of Music in the Creative Arts Center at West Virginia University,

and has been a high school band director.

He was instrumental in the formation of the West Virginia Trumpet Guild, an affiliate of the International Trumpet Guild, and served as the first president of that chapter. He has published several articles on trumpet teaching, has transcribed numerous works for solo trumpet and trumpet ensembles, and is widely known as a soloist and clinician.

Many of Mr. Sherman's students hold positions in professional symphony orchestras and armed service bands. In addition, several former students are teaching in respected schools and universities.

The Trumpeter's Handbook

A Comprehensive Guide to Playing and Teaching the Trumpet

by Roger Sherman

Accura Music Athens, Ohio 45701

ISBN: 0-918194-02-4

Library of Congress Catalog Card Number: LC 78-73020

Cover Design: Paul Bradford

Lithographed in the United States of America by Edwards Bros., Inc., Ann Arbor, Michigan

To *Susan, Jeffrey,* and *Stuart*

Acknowledgments

While it would be impractical to try to recognize everyone who assisted in a project of this magnitude, I feel I must note a few individuals who played a particularly large part in the completion of this book. My thanks go first to Dr. Reginald H. Fink, a friend who could see the possibility in undertaking this project and who was a continuing source of encouragement.

I appreciate the assistance of Richard Powell, trombone professor at West Virginia University, and Ruby Canning, WVU music librarian. Those having input in the technical aspects of the book include Lisa Cody, illustrator; Joel Cotter, copyist; Joan Gould, typist; Mildred Atkins, editorial consultant; and James Warner, photographer.

Thanks also to the Schilke, Yamaha, and Getzen instrument companies for technical assistance and examples, Accura Music, Charles Colin Music Publishing Co., The Brass Press, and Tromba Publications for permission to use illustrations and excerpts from publications, and Evco Embouchure Visualizers.

I must also add a note of thanks to my students through the years. We have shared in the solutions of their problems. With mutual understanding and patience, we have grown together.

Table of Contents

INTRODUCTION xv
1. HANDLING THE TRUMPET 1
    Opening the Case 1
    Inserting the Mouthpiece 1
    Oiling the Valves 1
    Emptying the Water Keys 2
2. HAND POSITION AND PLAYING POSITION 3
    Hand Grips 3
        Left Hand 3
        Right Hand 4
    Playing Position 5
    Position of the Music Stand 5
3. BREATHING 7
    Normal Breathing 7
    Inhalation for Trumpet Playing 8
    Inhalation Exercises 9
    Controlled Exhalation 9
    Catch Breaths 10
    Common Breathing Errors 10
4. THE EMBOUCHURE 12
    Dental Prerequisites 12
    Lip Formation 12
    Mouthpiece Placement 13
    The Chin 14
    The Embouchure Corners 15
    Stretching and Puckering 16
5. TONE PRODUCTION 19
    Lip Aperture 19
    Oral Cavaties 20
    Breath Supply and Support 20
    Open Throat 21
    Tonal Concept 21
    Tone Refinement 21
    Mouthpiece Pressure 21
    The Double Oscillation 21
6. ARTICULATION 23
    The Tongue 23
    The Function of the Tongue 23
    Tongue Placement 24
        Tip-Tonguing 24
        Dorsal-Tonguing 24
    Normal Articulation 24
    Note Lengths 26
    Accents 27
    Errors in Slurring 28
7. LEGATO PLAYING 30
    Lip Slurs 30
        Upward Slurs 30

x   Contents

      Downward Slurs. 31
      Lip Slur Errors 31
    Changing Valve Combinations 32
    Lip Flexibility Studies. 32
8. THE MOUTHPIECE. 34
    The Rim 34
    The Cup 34
    The Throat Shoulder and Orifice 34
    The Backbore 35
    The Shank 35
    Dirt. 35
    Plating 35
    Lucite or Plastic Mouthpieces. 35
    Changing Mouthpieces for Different Instruments 35
    Mouthpieces for the Beginner. 36
9. INSTRUMENT VARIABLES 37
    The Bore. 37
    The Bell 37
    Tuning Slide and Water Key 37
10. TRUMPET/CORNET DIFFERENCES 40
11. THE FLUGELHORN 42
12. THE C TRUMPET. 45
    Choosing a C Trumpet 47
    Adapting to the Instrument 47
    The C Cornet 47
13. THE HIGHER-KEY TRUMPETS. 49
    The D-E flat Trumpet. 49
    The F-G Trumpet 50
    The Piccolo A-B flat Trumpet. 52
    The Piccolo C Trumpet 53
    General Comments on Using the Fourth Valve on Higher Key Trumpets 54
14. SCALES AND ARPEGGIOS 56
    Memorization 56
    Diatonic Scale Patterns 56
    Simple and Compound Rhythmic Patterns 64
    Quintuplet Groupings 66
    Diminished Scales 67
    Whole Tone Scales 67
    Scales in Thirds and Pedal Points 68
    Arpeggios 68
      Tone Quality. 71
      Intonation 71
      Articulation 71
      High Register 71
      Low Register 71
      Endurance. 71
      Breath Control and Dynamics. 71
      Legato Control 71
15. VIBRATO 72
    Hand Vibrato 72
    Lip Vibrato 72
    Diaphragm Vibrato 72
    Vibrato in Various Registers 73

Teaching the Vibrato 73
Materials for Vibrato Practice 74
Vibrato Errors 74
16. TRANSPOSITION 75
Transposition in Applied Music 75
Transposition in Music Education 75
Transposition by Interval 75
Transposition by Clef 78
Clef Transpositions as Used on a B flat Trumpet 78
Beginning Teaching Steps 78
Piccolo A-B flat Trumpet Transpositions 80
17. MULTIPLE TONGUING 82
Teaching Multiple Tonguing 83
Flutter Tonguing 88
18. INTONATION ADJUSTMENTS 89
Valve Slide Relationships 89
Fifth Harmonic 89
Other Modes of Vibration 90
19. HOW TO PRACTICE 91
Preparation for the Warm-Up 91
The Warm-Up 91
Post Warm-Up Routine 93
Etude Practice 93
Review Material 93
New Material 93
Transposition 94
Solos and Excerpts 94
Endurance Exercises 94
The Warm-Down 95
20. SOLO AND AUDITION PREPARATION AND PERFORMANCE 97
Preparation 97
Performance Material 97
Mental Preparation 98
The Performance 99
Performance After a Wait 99
After the Performance 100
Etiquette 100
21. CONCERT DEPORTMENT IN ENSEMBLES 101
22. SELECTING THE APPROPRIATE INSTRUMENT 102
23. THE PROFESSIONAL ATTITUDE 118
24. DEVELOPING MUSICAL STYLE 119
25. MUTES 120
Straight Mute-Metal 120
Straight Mute-Fiber 120
Straight Mute-Plastic 121
Cup Mute 121
Wa-Wa or Harmon 121
Plunger 122
Hat, Metal Hat, or Derby 122
Felt Hat 122
Charlie Spivak "Whispa Mute" 123
Solotone Mute 123
Bucket 123

      Mutes for the Higher Key Trumpets 123
26. CONTEMPORARY TECHNIQUES 124
      Rhythmic Considerations 124
      Pitch Considerations 126
      Unconventional Sounds 129
27. FUNDAMENTAL REPAIR 130
      Cleaning the Mouthpiece 130
      Dents in the Mouthpiece 130
      Using the Cleaning Snake 130
      Valve Identification 131
      Valve Maintenance 131
      Removing a Frozen Slide 132
      Water Key Repair 133
      Using the Mouthpiece Puller 133
      Realizing Limitations 134
28. SELECTED LITERATURE 135
      Graded List of Literature and Technique 135
          Level 1 135
          Level 2 135
          Level 3 135
          Level 4 135
          Level 5 135
          Level 6 136
          Level 7 136
          Level 8 136
          Level 9 136
          Level 10 136
29. TRUMPET ENSEMBLES 137
30. INSTRUMENTS OF HISTORICAL INTEREST 138
      The Cornetto 138
      The Natural Trumpet 140
      The Keyed Trumpet 140
      Sources for Historical Instrument Reproductions 141
31. THE INTERNATIONAL TRUMPET GUILD 142
32. ANNOTATED BIBLIOGRAPHY 143

Table of Illustrations

Fig.   *Page*

 1. Oiling the Valves 1
 2. Emptying the Water Key 2
 3. Left Hand Position 3
 4. Left Hand Supporting the Trumpet 3
 5. Incorrect Thumb Position on the Trigger 3
 6. Correct Thumb Position on the Trigger 4
 7. Third Valve Slide Ring 4
 8. Left Hand—Pistol Grip 4
 9. Correct Right Hand Position 5
10. Incorrect Right Hand Position 5
11. Incorrect Left Arm Position 5
12. Playing Position with Music Stand—Standing 6
13. Playing Position with Music Stand—Seated 6
14. Diaphragm—Side View 7
15. Diaphragm—Front View 7
16. The Rib Cage 7
17. The Rib Cage and Intercostal Muscles 8
18. Breathing Through the Corners of the Mouth 9
19. Breath Control Exercise Using a Drinking Straw and a Glass of Water 10
20. Normal Overbite 12
21. Lip Formation—Front View 12
22. Lip Formation—Side View 13
23. Jaw Projected into Playing Position with the Mouthpiece 13
24. Lips Blowing Incorrectly into the Mouthpiece Cup 13
25. Embouchure Visualizer on the Lips 14
26. Lip Aperture Inside the Embouchure Visualizer 14
27. Embouchure Visualizer with Mirror 14
28. Pulling the Chin Down 15
29. Embouchure Visualizer with the Chin Puffed Incorrectly 15
30. The Embouchure Muscles 16
31. Touching the Corners of the Embouchure 16
32. Embouchure Muscles Stretched Incorrectly 16
33. Embouchure Muscles Puckered Incorrectly 17
34. Embouchure Mirror Attached to the Leadpipe 17
35. Blowing Through the Mouthpiece while Inserting it into the Instrument 19
36. Rolling a Finger over the End of the Mouthpiece 20
37. Top of the Tongue 23
38. Side of the Tongue—Flat Position 24
39. Side of the Tongue—Arched Position 24
40. The Mouthpiece 34
41. Mouthpiece Fit in Receiver 35
42. Space in Inner Bore Caused by Extending the Tuning Slide 38
43. Adjustable Tuning Bell 38
44. Water Key Cork with Nipple 38
45. Cross-Section of the Amado Water Key 39
46. Cornet and Trumpet Mouthpieces 40

47. Cornet and Trumpet 41
48. Flugelhorn 42
49. B flat and C Trumpets 45
50. Three Types of D Trumpets 49
51. Detail of Tuning Bell Trumpet 50
52. F-G Trumpet 50
53. Two Piccolo Trumpets 53
54. Piccolo C Trumpet 54
55. Right Hand Motion for Hand Vibrato 72
56. Jaw Motion for Lip Vibrato 73
57. Feeling the Air Impulse on the Hand 83
58. Straight Mutes 120
59. Other Mutes—Plunger, Bucket Cup, Whispa, Solotone. 121
60. Wa-Wa or Harmon Mute 121
61. Blowing Air into the Bell 122
62. Hat, Metal Hat, or Derby Mute 122
63. Folding Felt Envelope Mute 122
64. Felt Envelope Mute over Trumpet Bell 123
65. Half-Valve Technique 128
66. Using the Mouthpiece Brush 130
67. Removing a Dent from the Mouthpiece Shank 130
68. Cleaning Snake 131
69. Valve Guide. 131
70. Valve Cylinder Slots 131
71. Wiping the Valve 132
72. Cleaning the Cylinder. 132
73. Removing a Frozen Tuning Slide 132
74. Removing a Frozen Valve Slide 133
75. Using the Mouthpiece Puller 133
76. Cornetto and Cornettino 139
77. Cornetto Playing Position 139
78. Cornetto—Right Hand Position 139
79. Natural Trumpet 140
80. Keyed Trumpet 141

Introduction

The study of the applied aspect of any field refers to the practical use of ideas within that field for problem solving. Applied science incorporates laws, facts, and theories which allow engineers to build skyscrapers, bridges, and roads. Similarly, a finished musical performance is created by applying the knowledge of correct musical and technical aspects of performance on an instrument or group of instruments.

The study of applied music can be an exciting and rewarding experience for both the student and the teacher. Teachers usually find that no two students have the same problems or abilities. In this book I have presented many ideas which are relevant to the majority of individuals studying the trumpet. Some of these ideas may be conveyed effectively in a master class situation where the concepts are generally applicable to all students. Others must be dealt with on an individual basis.

This book, while making no pretense of being all things to all people, should be informative to most people within the music profession who are interested in quality trumpet teaching and performance. The thoughts presented herein have been culled from lessons with excellent private teachers who have been willing to share their knowledge, from authors of pedagogy books dealing with a wide variety of musical instruction, from conductors with creative musical ideas and the ability to develop them, and from 20 years of practical experience. I hope these concepts will have merit for band directors developing school music programs, for applied music teachers at the college level, and for serious students wishing to become better trumpet performers.

This book does not attempt to present a system, as is the vogue with many pedagogy books today. The principles endorsed are not necessarily unique to my teaching; many of them have been successfully utilized by other teachers. In cases where more than one technique could be used, I have attempted to present a cross section of ideas. The knowledgeable teacher should be prepared with alternative plans, where necessary, to deal with individual problems. As nothing is permanent, these thoughts have been altered and refined in my years of teaching and in all probability will be modified to some degree in the future.

Chapter 1

Handling the Trumpet

The conscientious teacher will want to be with beginning students when they have their first contact with the cornet or trumpet; otherwise, bad habits may be formed and set before the teacher has an opportunity to correct them. These initial habits are very difficult to change at a later date. It is essential to establish the proper holding position and embouchure at the beginning. In addition, a few minutes given to proper handling can prevent unnecessary damage.

Opening the Case

The case should be set on a secure surface, such as the floor or a table, before attempting to open it. Under no circumstance should the student try to balance the case with one arm while opening the clasps.

The student should be shown which way the case clasps open with the lid up. If the case is opened when inverted, there is a danger of the instrument falling out as very few instruments are secured into the case. Opening the case upside down could also allow the lyre or mouthpiece to fall against the instrument and cause a dent or scratch.

Inserting the Mouthpiece

How the mouthpiece is inserted might seem rather insignificant at first thought, but it is important to know how to insert the mouthpiece properly.

As the mouthpiece is inserted all the way into the mouthpiece receiver on the leadpipe, it should be turned slightly. Otherwise it may become stuck in the instrument. Never force or use excessive pressure when seating the mouthpiece in the receiver. Use care when removing a stuck mouthpiece as the solder joints on the leadpipe mounting braces may be broken. Mouthpiece removal is discussed in detail in Chapter 27, "Fundamental Repair."

Oiling the Valves

The valves should be oiled on a regular schedule so the action will always be the same. If not, the player places himself* at a disadvantage because it becomes

*It should be understood that when the masculine personal pronoun is used through this book, it is not intended to imply that only males are interested in the trumpet. On the contrary, there are females who are fine performers and teachers. The one gender is used only for writing ease.

impossible to work constructively when the valves are sticking. Another equally important reason for consistent oiling is to maintain a proper air seal within the piston mechanism of the instrument. When the valves are lubricated, there is less opportunity for air to escape around them and this will insure clean position changes between notes.

The oil should *never* be inserted through the hole in the bottom valve cap. All the dirt, corrosion, and organic material which runs down the valve collects in this cap. Oiling through this hole will wash any residue back up onto the piston causing it to stick and act as an abrasive on the valves and their casings. In time the abrasion from the dirt will wear the valves and casings out of round, thus making them leak air.

There are two acceptable ways to oil the valves. First, the most common and best way is to unscrew the top valve cap and lift the valve about half way out of the casing, enough so the piston is just exposed at the top of the cylinder. Put only one or two drops of oil on the piston and slide it back down into the cylinder. When putting the valve back in *do not rotate it;* push it in straight. Rotating or spinning the piston causes horizontal abrasion on the piston surface and in time these abrasions will prohibit the oil from spreading evenly over the valve.

Fig. 1 Oiling the Valves

1

This oiling procedure should be carried out with the instrument on the player's lap or with it lying securely on a table. Otherwise the player risks dropping the piston on the floor.

Second, an alternate way of oiling the valves is less effective, but there is less possibility of having an accident with the instrument. It is favored by some teachers of young beginning students for this reason. With this method a little oil is poured into the leadpipe before playing the instrument. Eventually the oil, together with water vapor, works its way around to the valves. The shortcomings of this system are that some of the oil is lost the first time the water key is opened, the pistons are operating without lubrication during the first few minutes of playing, and it is particularly difficult for the oil to pass around the leadpipe configuration of the cornet.

There are several commercial brands of valve oil available in music stores. These oils may vary in efficiency depending on the make and model of instrument and the conditions under which it is played. An acceptable (and less expensive) substitute is kerosene. If the smell of the straight kerosene is too offensive, a few drops of peppermint extract or tincture of wintergreen may be added. Ten drops of olive oil per pint of kerosene will add to its adhesion to the valves. It may be necessary to experiment with this ratio as its effectiveness may vary with the age of the instrument and the valve tolerance.

Emptying the Water Keys

All instruments have a water key on the bottom of the first crook of the leadpipe. Many also have one on the third valve slide. Most of the water collects

Fig. 2 Emptying the Water Key

in the leadpipe and it is a simple procedure to get it out. The water key is opened and the player blows air into the mouthpiece.

It is sometimes more difficult to get water out of the third valve slide, although less will accumulate there. Usually it is necessary to push the third valve down while the water key is open and air is being blown through the instrument.

Chapter 2
Hand Position and Playing Position

Correct hand position is of utmost importance when playing the cornet and trumpet. If the instrument is held incorrectly this can be a source of tension and discomfort and can impair successful progress.

Left Hand

The left hand is positioned so the bell of the instrument rests on the first knuckle of the index finger and the knuckle of the thumb. The left hand thus forms a cradle which balances the instrument.

Fig. 4 Left Hand Supporting the Trumpet

the right thumb causes tension in that hand and interferes with smooth finger operation of the valves.

There is a ring on the third valve slide on most instruments. Some manufacturers make this adjustable

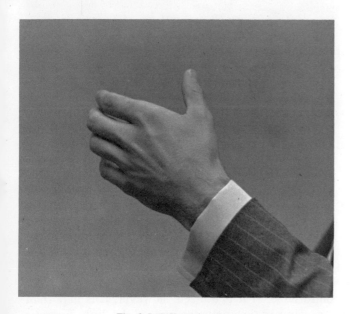

Fig. 3 Left Hand Position

It is important to remember that the fingers do not grip the valves. Gripping can cause tension in the left hand and arm and ultimately lead to pulling back, thus making excessive pressure with the mouthpiece on the embouchure. It is more correct to think of the fingers as being wrapped around the valves in a relaxed manner.

The instrument may have a thumb saddle or trigger on the first valve slide, which is used to adjust the tuning of certain fingering combinations. (See Chapter 18, "Intonation Adjustments" for a detailed discussion of the use of triggers and thumb saddles.) In some cases the brace for the trigger is offset to the right of the first valve cylinder. Even if this is the case, the trigger is still operated by the *left* thumb. Using

Fig. 5 Incorrect Thumb Position on the Trigger

Fig. 6 Correct Thumb Position on the Trigger

by having a bar on the ring which slides through a sleeve with a set screw. This allows the ring to be moved to accommodate various hand sizes.

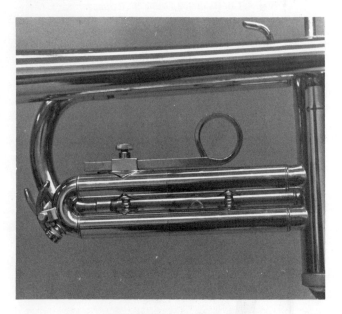

Fig. 7 Third Valve Slide Ring

Regardless of whether the ring is permanently attached or adjustable, the fourth finger must be used. This permits the third finger to assist in pushing the third valve slide out when it is used for tuning adjustments. In the same manner, the little finger is used in drawing the slide back in.

Some players use a pistol grip left hand position. While it may be argued that a few professional players use this and are highly successful, it is not a universally accepted method. Utilization of the third valve slide is restricted and the stretched position of the fingers makes left arm relaxation difficult.

Fig. 8 Left Hand—Pistol Grip

Right Hand

The right thumb is placed below the leadpipe where the first and second valve cylinders meet. The hook for the little finger on the leadpipe may or may not be used, depending on what the player finds most comfortable. If it is utilized, however, it is important to remember that only the end of the little finger is placed in it. If the little finger is inserted too far, the three middle fingers operating the valves will be too far over the valve caps to give clear finger articulation.

The fingers operating the valves should be positioned in a gentle arch, almost as if a softball were being held in the palm of the hand. The position of the fingertips on the valve caps should allow the right hand and arm to remain relaxed. This position may vary somewhat between players, but the ultimate concern should be a complete absence of tension.

Care should be exercised to press the fingers directly on the top of the valve cap, not the side. Over a period of time pressing on the side can wear the valves unevenly and cause them to bind and leak.

The fingers should remain in contact with the caps even when the valves are not depressed. It is impossible

Fig. 9 Correct Right Hand Position

Fig. 10 Incorrect Right Hand Position

to operate the pistons smoothly if the fingers are suspended in the air away from the valve caps.

Playing Position

Proper posture is essential when playing the trumpet in either a standing or sitting position. The instrument is brought to the player, rather than the player jutting the head forward to meet the mouthpiece. When the trumpet is in playing position the spine should be straight and the neck and head must be a continuation of this line.

The arms should be away from the body so the torso is free to expand for the most efficient use of the breath. This is especially important when playing seated. Many players will rest their left arms against their bodies when they get tired and this restricts the breath flow and support.

Fig. 11 Incorrect Left Arm Position

The player should remember not to *lean* against the back of the chair or slouch. This would hamper taking in an adequate amount of air.

Whether the player is standing or sitting the instrument should be tilted so the bell is approximately 15 degrees below a line parallel with the floor.

Position of the Music Stand

The music stand should be positioned so that when the performer is holding the instrument in playing position, the trumpet bell will be even with the bottom of the page. The instrument should be directed slightly off to either the right or left of the stand so that the tone quality will not be distorted by having an object in front of the bell.

In ensembles there should be no more than two players per music stand. If more than two try to crowd

Fig. 12 Playing Position with Music Stand—Standing

Fig. 13 Playing Position with Music Stand—Seated

around one stand some players will develop a crouching or twisted posture and a distorted embouchure. The director should buy extra music rather than jeopardize his teaching results by neglecting to get enough music and stands.

Chapter 3
Breathing

The importance of understanding the physical concepts of breathing cannot be overemphasized. A student may have mastered all the other basic techniques of the instrument, but if the breathing is incorrect, he cannot play with a good tone.

The breath actually represents the foundation of musical tone for wind players. When students breathe correctly, they are able to work toward refinement of other playing techniques knowing they are building on a secure base.

Normal Breathing

We must first examine how a person breathes normally to understand what adjustments are necessary for the trumpet student. The trunk of the body is divided into two major sections—the thoracic cavity and the abdominal cavity. The two cavities are separated by a large dome-shaped muscle called the diaphragm.

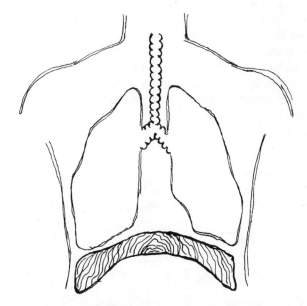

Fig. 15 Diaphragm—Front View

so that it may expand and contract. There are five pairs of ribs which are attached to the sternum in front with cartilage, five more pairs below these which attach the same way but do not extend completely around to the front, and two additional pairs called "floating ribs," which attach only to the backbone.

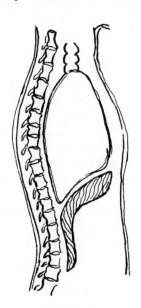

Fig. 14 Diaphragm—Side View

The heart and lungs are within the thoracic cavity. They are enclosed by the rib cage which is a combination of bone and cartilage. The ribs are attached to the backbone with cartilage. The rib cage is rigid enough to protect these vital organs, yet the cartilage joining the bones makes the whole structure flexible enough

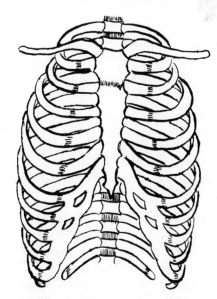

Fig. 16 The Rib Cage

The rib cage is laced together with a fibrous sheath called intercostal muscles. There are two types of these intercostals. The external intercostals are attached to the outside of the rib cage. The fibres of these muscles are directed downwards and forwards. These cover the rib cage as far forward as the bony part of the ribs where the cartilage begins in the front. The internal intercostals are attached to the inside of the rib cage and the fibres are directed downwards and backwards. There are two types of internal intercostals. Those which attach to the five pairs of ribs where they join the sternum are called the intercartilaginous internal intercostal muscles. Continuing around the inside of the rib cage are the interosseous internal intercostal muscles.

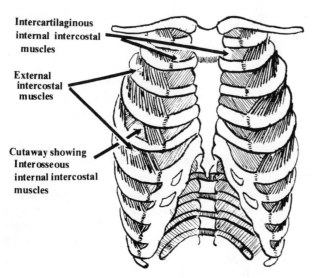

Intercartilaginous internal intercostal muscles

External intercostal muscles

Cutaway showing Interosseous internal intercostal muscles

Fig. 17 The Rib Cage and Intercostal Muscles

There is some controversy as to the exact function of these different muscles. From the standpoint of physiology for the musician, the following should adequately describe the respective roles of these muscles:

1. The external intercostals and the intercartilaginous internal intercostals contract and lift the rib cage outward and upward and function during inhalation.
2. The interosseous internal intercostals contract and draw the rib cage down and back and function during exhalation.

Immediately below the diaphragm in the abdominal cavity are the liver, the gall bladder and the stomach, and below these, the large and small intestines. The dome-shaped diaphragm is a muscle which flattens when contracted and compresses against the organs in the abdominal cavity. The process of normal breathing consists of two simultaneous steps. The diaphragm contracts at the same time that the external intercostals and the intercartilaginous internal intercostals raise and expand the rib cage. These two actions create a partial vacuum. Air entering the nose and mouth fills the lungs to equalize the air pressure on the inside and the outside of the thoracic cavity. The normal exhalation of air involves contracting the interosseous internal intercostals and relaxation of the diaphragm to its normal arched position. The repetition of this vital involuntary cycle goes unnoticed by most individuals throughout their lives.

Inhalation for Trumpet Playing

The amount of air used in normal breathing is not sufficient to produce a tone on a trumpet. It is imperative that we increase appreciably the amount of air inhaled and we must also develop a way to control its release.

The easiest way to take a large breath rapidly is through the mouth. It is helpful to remain as relaxed as possible and strive to duplicate the same approach as that used with a normal breath. All points of resistance, for example, the lips, teeth, tongue, and throat, must be kept as open as possible. The jaw drops and the tongue is lowered to the bottom of the mouth so the oral cavity is fully open. The throat and neck remain relaxed. Some teachers advocate thinking of having a piece of hot food in the back of the mouth and quickly drawing air in to cool it.

The muscles of the abdominal wall relax to allow the organs below the diaphragm to drop as far as possible in the body cavity. This relaxation in turn allows the diaphragm to more fully contract and drop further. The thoracic cavity is then expanded from the bottom upward and outward. The sternum is in a lifted position and this allows the top of the lungs to fill as a final step.

It is important to note that the shoulders do not rise in this complete breathing process. Nothing can be added to the lung capacity by raising the shoulders and it only serves to make the neck and shoulders more tense.

The trumpeter will often be able to take large breaths through the mouth as described above. It is also important to develop the ability to breathe through the corners of the mouth while the mouthpiece is still in place on the embouchure. This allows the air supply to be replenished with only a minimal interruption of the musical line. The corners of the mouth are used, rather than the nose, for two reasons. First, a great volume of air can be taken in more quickly through the mouth. Second, the change in the embouchure corners when inhaling allows fresh blood to flow through the embouchure muscles. Oxygen which is present in this blood revitalizes the muscles supporting the mouthpiece. A combination of these muscles flexing and the oxygen supply can increase endurance significantly. Holding the corners rigid and breathing through the nose is similar to cutting off the blood supply to a finger by tying a string around it. It is not necessary to completely remove the mouthpiece from the lips. Releasing the mouthpiece pressure and opening the corners of the mouth is sufficient to renew the blood supply.

Fig. 18 Breathing Through the Corners of the Mouth

Inhalation Exercises

There are numerous exercises available for practicing deep breathing. The following five examples are suggested by Reginald H. Fink in *The Trombonist's Handbook,* the trombone counterpart to this book.

1. While standing erect, breathe fully and raise the arms outward from the sides to a position parallel with the floor. Hold the inhalation and return the arms to the sides. Notice the expanded lower rib cage.
2. While seated, bend over and grasp one ankle. Inhale and note the expansion of the lower ribs and the contraction of the muscles of the lower back.
3. Notice, while lying on your back on the floor, how during normal breathing the abdomen rises and falls. In the same position, inhale as deeply as possible and note the expansion of both the lower rib cage and the abdomen.

4. Without being concerned with the expansion, inhale while thinking of drawing the air along the bottom of the mouth. On successive inhalations where the air is drawn along the bottom of the mouth, note the expansion of the lower ribs and the abdomen. A similar idea is to breathe while thinking of inhaling a pleasant vapor.
5. Edward Kleinhammer in *The Art of Trombone Playing* recommends that the player always be aware of the additional breath that can be taken. To increase your capacity, you should fully inhale and then take in even a bit more breath. Hardly anyone finds that the first inhalation is truly complete. There is always space for a little more air.

Still another set of exercises is recommended by Philip Farkas in *The Art of Brass Playing.* He suggests practicing the two main functions of the inhalation process in separate steps. The diaphragm is forcefully contracted to lower it while the rib cage remains stationary. After the maximum intake is reached with the diaphragm alone, the rib cage is lifted and expanded. The steps are then reversed so the thoracic cavity expands first. When its maximum is reached, the diaphragm is contracted. The steps are then combined to achieve one long, continuous inhalation.

All of these exercises serve to sharpen awareness of what an individual is assisted in doing by nature itself. Most people take the breathing process so much for granted that they cannot describe it. When inhaling the maximum capacity of air, the goal should be to achieve this by relaxing as much as possible. If the abdominal muscles are tensed while trying to lower the diaphragm to its fullest, the only result will be strain and possible injury.

Controlled Exhalation

Once the maximum amount of air has been inhaled, we encounter problems which are not common with normal exhalation. Everyone has seen what happens when a balloon is inflated to its fullest and then released. If it is large enough there are three distinct steps to the air release. During the first stage it flies haphazardly, jumping erratically from one place to another. Then there is a short period when the balloon actually flies with some control. The final stage occurs when there is too little air within to keep the balloon supported. It falls to the floor and makes a few movements before coming to rest.

The last phase of this analogy does not concern us because the final stages of breath exhalation are not adequate to maintain a trumpet tone. The first two do have some points of interest to the problems of trumpet playing.

During the first stage of exhalation the air is difficult to control because there is a natural tendency for the player to want to get rid of air that exceeds the amount taken with a normal breath. The student who has not mastered control of exhalation will tend to play loudly immediately following the breath, regardless of the dynamic. The articulations will often be much stronger than is musically correct.

Physical resistance on the part of the performer must be kept to a minimum. The chest must not be constricted and the throat stays open. It is especially important to keep the teeth separated. There are three points of resistance which exist in all situations: the lip aperture, the mouthpiece throat, and the instrument. If a high note is being played, a fourth point, the arched tongue, provides additional resistance. If the note is in the middle or low range the tongue should remain flat in the bottom of the mouth so that there will be no additional resistance. This concept of tongue position is discussed in detail in Chapter 7, "Legato Playing."

The first phase of the exhalation takes place because of the contracting of the interosseous internal intercostal muscles and the rising of the diaphragm as it returns to its relaxed state. These muscles cannot be permitted to make this transition too quickly or the player will have no control of the air.

The second phase of the exhalation involves an entirely different set of problems than the first phase. After the surplus of air is cleared from the thoracic cavity, the remaining amount of air necessary for a note or phrase must be pushed out of the cavity. There are numerous ideas as to how this should be accomplished. We know that it is impossible to push the diaphragm up because it is merely an involuntary muscle in the natural process of relaxation when we are exhaling. We can, however, lift the internal organs below the diaphragm by firming the muscles in the abdominal wall. Various ideas may encourage sucking in or pushing out, but it is my feeling that the concept of lifting the diaphragm is much more appropriate (and safer) than encouraging muscle rigidity in the abdominal area.

It is also important to note that the thoracic cavity does not compress and push the air out. Thinking compression only results in a forced tone.

Dr. Fink suggests blowing through a straw into a drinking glass half filled with water. The object of this is to maintain a steady flow of bubbles. This is most difficult at the point where there is a transition from the relaxed exhalation to the supported exhalation. This

Fig. 19 Breath Control Exercise Using a Drinking Straw and a Glass of Water

gives the player a visible idea of the rate of air flow. It becomes more even and controlled with practice.

Catch Breaths

It is essential that trumpet players master the catch breath, to use in circumstances when there is a continuous musical line. With careful analysis and planning the performer can decide where it is possible to sneak in a quick breath without disturbing the musical line.

The catch breath is not just an ordinary musical breath executed more quickly. There are two important differences. There is obviously a continuation of the musical phrase following a catch breath. The breath support from the abdominal muscles remains constant during the intake. For this reason, the bulk of the breath is drawn in by the expansion of the thoracic cavity. The second difference relates to the speed the embouchure corners must open and close. They must open enough to take in an adequate supply of air, but the closing occurs a mere split second later. The mouthpiece remains in place on the embouchure during both normal and catch breaths.

Common Breathing Errors

There are a few common errors which students make that can hamper good breath control. The first mistake that is quite common is to hesitate between the inhalation and the exhalation. Many students will pause for a split second because of a feeling of apprehension. This pause only exaggerates the problem. Ideally one should attempt to duplicate the normal function of breathing as closely as possible. The hesitation not only interrupts the even flow of air, but also makes the following articulation disproportionately loud.

The second most common fault of many students is not to breathe often enough. When sustaining a long note on the trumpet, there comes a point when it is possible to detect a change in tone quality as the player tenses his body as he tries to force the note to continue. To sustain the line without tension, one or more breaths must be added. The melodic line should be analyzed to find the most appropriate places for breathing in relation to dynamics, phrases, and range.

Another common fault relates to the previous point. All breaths are not of equal size. Students should look at the phrase carefully to determine how much air is necessary to sustain the passage securely, then take in slightly more than that amount. The extra air represents a small security reserve in case of nervousness or slight alteration in the tempo.

Taking maximum breaths all the time is just as harmful as not breathing often enough, as the body becomes bloated with the stale air left in the lungs after partial exhalation.

All the physiological detail involved with successful breath control for trumpet playing might seem to be overly complex. Indeed, a student is very lucky if he does not have to relate to these ideas, but merely comes by correct breathing naturally. For those who are not as fortunate, it should be sufficient to give an explanation of the function of the involuntary muscles with some detail regarding necessary modifications for the trumpet.

Chapter 4
The Embouchure

The trumpeter's embouchure is probably the most discussed aspect of playing the instrument. While correct formation of the embouchure and mouthpiece placement on the embouchure are quite important, they should not be treated as age-old secrets known to only a few gifted individuals. When proper rules for embouchure formation are observed, students and teachers will share in rewarding musical experiences.

Dental Prerequisites

Most people have a small overbite. The top teeth of these individuals extend slightly beyond the bottom teeth when the lower jaw is closed so that the upper and lower molars meet comfortably.

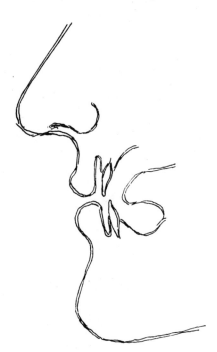

Fig. 20 Normal Overbite

Slight discrepancies in tooth formation do not adversely affect an individual's success with the trumpet. Care should be taken, however, to avoid selecting a student who will surely need orthodontic work.

The time when an orthodontist chooses to apply braces invariably coincides with that period when the student is just beginning to have some success with the instrument. While it is possible to play the trumpet with braces by using beeswax applications to the metal wires, there is usually a very distinct change in tone quality, flexibility, and endurance. These factors tend to depress even the most enthusiastic student.

Lip Formation

There are three basic steps in forming the lips into an acceptable trumpet embouchure. First, moisten the lips slightly and with the lips lightly closed, extend the lower jaw so the top and bottom teeth are aligned.

At this point the lips should be in a position as if they were saying a closed *M*, as in "me."

Fig. 21 Lip Formation—Front View

Steps two and three occur at the same time. With the jaw in the projected position (step one), separate the teeth about a quarter of an inch and at the same time, while keeping the lips together, roll the lips in slightly.

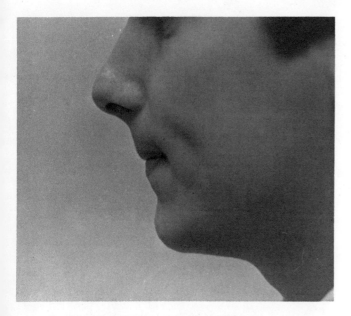

Fig. 22 Lip Formation—Side View

Mouthpiece Placement

Once the lips are in the correct position, the mouthpiece may be set on the lips.

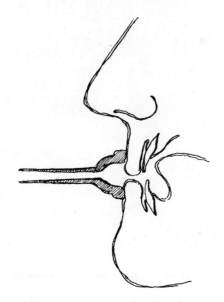

Fig. 23 Jaw Projected Into Playing Position with the Mouthpiece

The horizontal placement of the mouthpiece on the lips should be as close to the center as possible. The only factor necessitating a location other than center might be some misalignment in one of the front teeth. Having the mouthpiece centered horizontally allows the

muscles on both sides of the face to share equally in supporting the embouchure.

The vertical mouthpiece placement may vary between one-third upper lip and two-thirds lower lip, to one-half upper lip and one-half lower lip. Of these two alternatives, the one-third/two-third distribution seems to be more universally accepted. It is generally agreed that moving the mouthpiece downward on the lips causes the tone quality to be more brilliant. As this is the common concept of trumpet tone, it stands to reason this distribution would be recognized as the most acceptable within the limits of individual differences.

After the student has found a location that feels comfortable he should remove and replace the mouthpiece in that location a few times. It is helpful if the lips are moist throughout this practice as the moisture will make it easier to find the same place consistently.

Moistening the embouchure is a necessity for all students throughout their training. If both the lips and the mouthpiece are dry on contact, the mouthpiece invariably will stick to the spot it touches first, rather than find the established position.

Next, the student should blow through the mouthpiece to get the feeling of keeping the lips rolled in. A common fault with beginning students is to relax the lips when they begin blowing. If the lips are allowed to relax, the embouchure will collapse and the lips are blown toward the mouthpiece cup. When the inner surface of the lips does the vibrating there will be no control of the sound and the tone is airy and distorted.

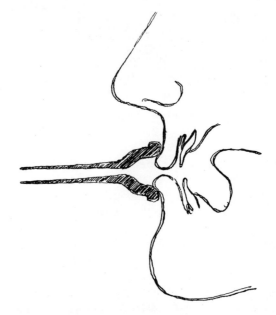

Fig. 24 Lips Blowing Incorrectly into the Mouthpiece Cup

Blowing freely through the mouthpiece with the lips rolled in slightly should create an opening (aperture) through which the air passes. No attempt should be made at this point to make the lips buzz. (This is discussed extensively in Chapter 5, "Tone Production.") A buzz may be produced, but whether or not it is present when playing the trumpet should not be of prime importance at this point.

If there is no air passing between the lips, it is quite likely that the lips are rolled in too far. When the lips are rolled in excessively, the air behind the lips actually blows them tightly together and obstructs the passage of air into the mouthpiece.

It would be wise at this time for the teacher to check the mouthpiece location with an embouchure visualizer, which is nothing more than a mouthpiece rim mounted on a metal rod. When the mouthpiece location is duplicated with the visualizer, the upper and lower lip distribution will be obvious.

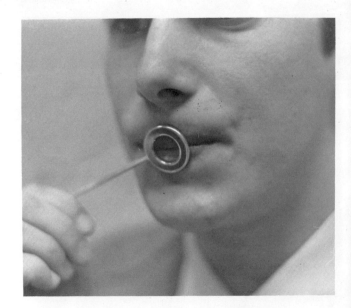

Fig. 26 Lip Aperture Inside the Embouchure Visualizer

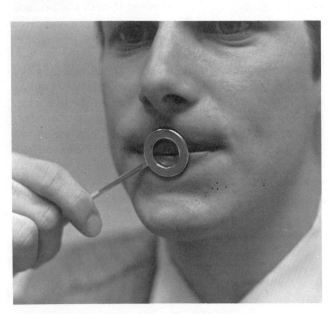

Fig. 25 Embouchure Visualizer on the Lips

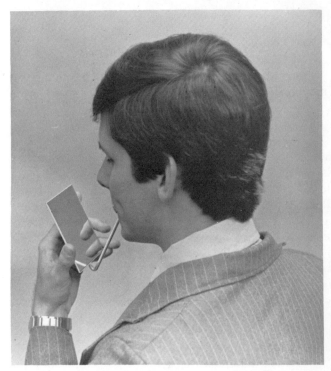

Fig. 27 Embouchure Visualizer with Mirror

If the placement is correct, the student can blow through the visualizer to establish the lip aperture, being careful again not to let the embouchure collapse, allowing the lips to extend into the visualizer.

A recent innovation in commercially available embouchure visualizers is a visualizer with a mirror attached.

This visualizer allows the student to check his own embouchure placement and aperture formation. The visualizer is used with a beginning student only occasionally after the correct placement is established. It

should not be necessary for the beginner to check placement constantly unless the teacher is making some adjustment.

The Chin

The upper part of the chin remains flat when the correct trumpet embouchure is set. This feeling can be simulated by placing the forefinger of one hand across the chin with the thumb underneath the chin. Have the student pull down on his chin as if there were a goatee.

Fig. 28 Pulling the Chin Down

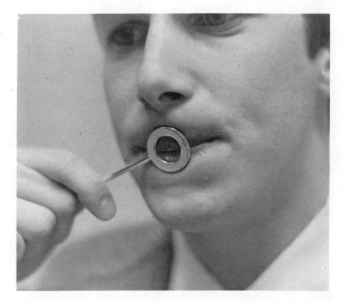

Fig. 29 Embouchure Visualizer with the Chin Puffed Incorrectly

Two common problems facing trumpet players are avoided when the chin remains flat. The first problem is the tendency to let an air pocket form between the lower gum and the front of the chin. Some students think that an air pocket here gives them a feeling of additional cushion for the mouthpiece. While there might be some temporary comfort from this technique, it can have damaging long range effects. If an air bubble is allowed to form under the lower lip, the continuity of muscle support will not be consistent around the embouchure, the top lip will be firmer than the bottom, and the lower half of the aperture will be uncontrolled.

The second reason for keeping the chin flat is to avoid the pitfall of letting the lower lip roll inward too far. As noted before, it is necessary to roll both lips in *slightly* when forming the embouchure, but some students will roll the lower lip too much. There is a *little* temporary assistance when ascending into the upper register if the lower lip is rolled in more than normal. The long-range effect, however, will be quite harmful as the aperture is pinched closed in the process. The tone becomes thinner and the maximum high range actually is limited severely. Some students even go to the extreme of rolling the bottom lip in over the lower teeth. Any attempt to assist the upper register

production with this technique will have detrimental results and should be avoided. (Procedures for building the upper register are discussed under lip slurs in Chapter 7, "Legato Playing.")

The Embouchure Corners

The corners of the embouchure should remain secure, but not be held in a rigid manner. The muscle that surrounds the lips, the muscles at the corners of the mouth, those in the cheeks, neck, and chin, all converge in the corners of the embouchure. If these muscles do not function properly, the embouchure will not be supported properly.

This muscle support increases as the range goes higher, but is also necessary when playing in the low register of the trumpet. If the embouchure support lapses in the lower range, the pitches will be flat and the tone will not match the timbre of the middle and upper register.

Inconsistent embouchure support also will allow the cheeks to puff. This lack of embouchure control causes the tone to be uncentered and severely limits endurance.

The added air velocity necessary for the upper register may also puff out the upper lip. This puffing is another symptom of incomplete embouchure muscle support.

When the student lets the muscle support of the embouchure corners lapse, the teacher can lightly place a finger at the point where the muscles converge. The touch usually serves as enough of a reminder to the student that the muscles become set correctly again.

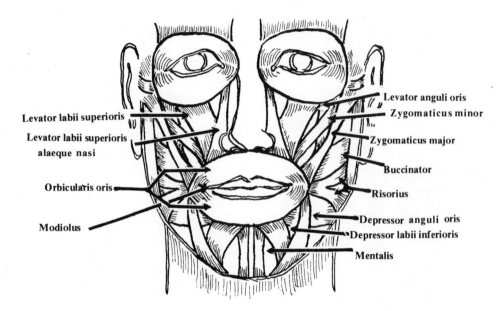

Fig. 30 The Embouchure Muscles

Fig. 31 Touching the Corners of the Embouchure

Stretching and Puckering

Through the years there have been several varying ways of setting the embouchure muscles for trumpet playing. One system endorsed the idea that the corners of the embouchure should be drawn back as the player ascended into the high register, thus stretching the lips across the teeth. The theory behind this thinking stated that as the lips became thinner, they vibrated faster. There are two major shortcomings to this idea. There

is a limit to how far the corners of the embouchure can be drawn back and as the lips become thinner there is less muscle tissue between the mouthpiece and the teeth. Consequently the embouchure becomes fatigued quickly.

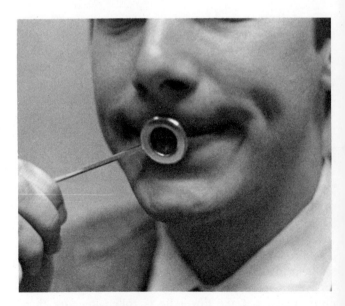

Fig. 32 Embouchure Muscles Stretched Incorrectly

The counterpart to this idea was the suggestion that one should bunch more muscle tissue between the teeth and the mouthpiece by drawing the corners of the embouchure in towards the center.

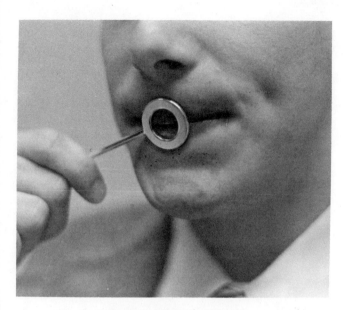

Fig. 33 Embouchure Muscles Puckered Incorrectly

This puckering technique also has shortcomings. The tone quality changes with the thickness of the tissue and there is some loss of flexibility.

Other teachers have advocated a combination of these two techniques. The muscles in the center of the embouchure are drawn together while the corners are stretched back. This rigid setting often inhibits upper range and limits flexibility. None of these systems are taught with any widespread acceptance these days.

Conclusion

Instrumental music teachers may be saying, "All this is well and good, but I have too many students to look after and cannot spend this amount of time on embouchure." To these teachers I would make the following points:

1. Establishing the correct embouchure during the initial lessons is the most important commitment you can make. It will have a direct relationship to each student's success in a music program.
2. Successful school music programs should not be based upon survival of the most adaptable, or the luckiest. Solid programs are based on knowledgeable teaching.
3. Correct embouchure can be taught just as effectively (sometimes more effectively) in a class situation. If students are aware of difficulties their peers are having and can see them corrected, they are likely to be much more aware of correct embouchure formation and function.

4. While it may seem that several steps are necessary in embouchure preparation, a beginning student can pick up these ideas in very few minutes. Compare this to the hours of frustration encountered by a student who finds that it is necessary to change the embouchure after several years of playing with an incorrect one.

There are two other points which I feel are relevant to band directors and successful embouchure teaching. There should *never* be more than two students playing from a single music stand, or some students will be forced to change their vertical placement so they can read the music more easily. A shortage of music stands invariably creates problems.

Many band directors recruit their French horn players by converting their more successful trumpet students. Many times they do not stop to think that the reason that those players are successful is because they are playing on the correct embouchure. The same mouthpiece placement will not be successful on the French horn. It would be better to look for a trumpet player who has the mouthpiece placed too high on the embouchure. This student could quite possibly play on the same embouchure which was not satisfactory on the trumpet and find it might be successful on the French horn.

Teachers should be aware that it is essential to have a mirror handy for students who are working with mouthpiece placement. This is true both in the beginning stages of study and in remedial work. A cosmetic mirror

Fig. 34 Embouchure Mirror Attached to the Leadpipe

may be placed on the music stand. The stand is then adjusted for correct visual alignment. A more recent development is the embouchure mirror which may be temporarily clamped to the trumpet leadpipe.

Either of these mirror arrangements will enable the student to examine the mouthpiece placement and see the functioning of the embouchure muscles. The mirror should not be used throughout a student's daily practicing, but only during the periods when embouchure study is desired.

Chapter 5
Tone Production

When all of the elements of trumpet performance are evaluated, the one aspect which becomes the most important concern is tone quality. The success of the total musical impression is contingent on the tone. A rapid articulation, exceptional range, or flashy technique means nothing if the tone is unsatisfactory while executing any of these.

There are various factors which relate to the tone quality that a person will produce on an instrument. This quality is unique with every player and two individuals playing the same instrument and the same mouthpiece could quite possibly produce two different tone qualities. Factors which make the difference are the size and shape of the oral cavity, the breath supply and how well it is supported, the openness of the throat, and the lip aperture.

Lip Aperture or "To Buzz or Not to Buzz"

I consider the lip aperture the most important and will discuss it first because it relates to students at all levels of advancement. The subject of lip aperture is presented at the beginning student's first attempt to produce a tone on the trumpet.

Dr. Arthur H. Benade, in *Fundamentals of Musical Acoustics,* compares the lips of the brass player with the singer's vocal cords. In either case, this is the point where the tone oscillation takes place.

When beginning students are introduced to trumpet tone production, invariably the teacher tells them to buzz their lips to produce the tone. (One widely accepted trumpet pedagogy book has the students buzz the lips alone for a week, buzz the lips into the mouthpiece for a week, and finally produce a tone on the instrument in the third week.) Buzzing either with the lips alone, with a visualizer, or on the mouthpiece by itself requires one lip surface to be vibrated *against* the other.

It is my contention that the lips do vibrate in the air stream, but a more free, open tone can be produced by keeping the aperture larger and not forcing the lips to strike each other as they do when they buzz. The following experiment can illustrate this principle:

1. Buzz a third space C on the mouthpiece. While sustaining this pitch, bring the trumpet toward the mouthpiece and slowly insert the mouthpiece into

the receiver. Naturally, a third space C will sound.

2. Now enlarge the lip aperture within the mouthpiece so there is no buzz, but use the same air velocity and the same embouchure muscle support. Again bring the instrument slowly to the mouthpiece. The third space C will sound when the mouthpiece is one-half to two-thirds into the receiver.

Fig. 35 Blowing Through the Mouthpiece while Inserting it into the Instrument

3. Reverse the procedure and remove the mouthpiece from the instrument while playing the pitch. The opposite of steps one and two will occur. When the more open aperture is used as in step 2, the tone will stop when the mouthpiece is approximately one-third to one-half out of the receiver. There will be no buzz sounded, only the air moving through the mouthpiece. When executing the reverse of step 1, the buzz will continue with the mouthpiece alone. The demonstration may go one step farther at this point. If the mouthpiece is removed from the lips during the production of the buzz in step 1, the lips will continue the buzzing sound because of the tight aperture.

4. While holding the mouthpiece alone, use the more open aperture with the same air velocity and embouchure muscle support, and blow through the mouthpiece. Hold the index finger of the other hand below the open shank end of the mouthpiece. Gradually roll the index finger over the open hole. When the hole is covered one-half to two-thirds by the index finger, a third space C will begin to buzz audibly.

Fig. 36 Rolling a Finger over the end of the Mouthpiece

5. Roll the finger down and the buzz stops, leaving only the sound of air passing through the lip aperture into the mouthpiece.

In both cases the sound is generated by the oscillation of the lips. Similarly, in both cases the lips open and close. This can be perceived by doing the same experiment using a transparent mouthpiece. (It may be easier to see the results with a trombone mouthpiece because the larger curve to the cup does not cause as much distortion to the view.) With the open aperture, the tone begins (or the buzz starts when the mouthpiece alone is used) when resistance is added to the air flow. The resistance causes a reflection in the standing waves present in the instrument (or mouthpiece alone) and causes the lip aperture to close as part of the oscillation.

A more open tone can be produced with the more open aperture. I would not be foolish enough to believe this concept will work for *all* players. I have seen first hand, however, that many trumpet students *will* improve their sound significantly by opening the aperture more in this manner.

The results of this experiment may be even more appropriate for the beginning student. It should not be necessary to insist that students buzz the lips or the mouthpiece as the initial step in playing the instrument. I have started beginners with very positive results using this concept and found that it was unnecessary to ever mention buzzing to produce the tone. The only time it is necessary to resort to a discussion of buzzing is when the student gets only the sound of air rushing through the instrument. In this case it is obvious that the lip aperture is too large and the lips need to be placed closer together.

Oral Cavities

The tonal resonance is enhanced by enlarging the oral cavity as much as possible. To do this the teeth must be kept separated and the lower jaw must be pulled down. The tongue should also remain in the bottom of the mouth as if singing the syllable *aah*. Note: It may be impossible to incorporate this lowered tongue when playing in the high register because it is essential that the tongue be arched to increase the air velocity for the high range.

The performer must play in the center of the tone to get the best timbre. The center of the tone is that area where the tone has a characteristic brilliant quality, yet is firm and resonant. Playing above the tone center will result in a quality which is too brilliant and lacks resonance. The area below the tone center has a quality which is too dull. Students should strive to find the tone center in each pitch on the trumpet. With a fine instrument the resonance will usually coincide with that point where the intonation is also correct. If the intonation is not correct at the resonance point, then tuning adjustments or alternate fingerings must be used.

Breath Supply and Support

A good trumpet tone is produced with a combination of support and relaxation. Support, however, must not be confused with tension, since tension has no place in good tone production. The support is derived from the abdominal wall muscles pushing the internal organs below the diaphragm and lifting it which in turn supports the air column. This is coordinated with the support of the embouchure muscles.

It is essential to relax the diaphragm muscles, the intercostal muscles surrounding the chest cavity, the muscles of the neck, shoulders, throat, and the tongue.

(Elaboration of these points may be found in Chapter 3, "Breathing" and Chapter 4, "Embouchure.")

Open Throat

Tension in the throat will make it impossible to produce a free, resonant tone. It is helpful to think of maintaining an unobstructed passage as you would when singing. Likewise, it is important to keep the neck and shoulders relaxed, as tension there will also distort the tone quality.

Tonal Concept

One cannot overemphasize how important it is for students to hear examples of good trumpet tone on recordings, in live performances of respected players, and from examples played by the private teacher. If students are not able to hear the difference between good tone quality and that which is unacceptable, there is very little chance that they will have any success on the instrument.

Tone Refinement

Long tone and lip slur practice are essential in the development and refinement of tone production. When playing long tones, students should be very aware that the tone quality must be consistent throughout the dynamic range of the instrument. Many students can produce a tone which is quite acceptable in the *piano* (*p*) through *mezzo-forte* (*mf*) dynamic range. Beyond that point the sound tends to become harsh. The harsh quality is caused partially because the muscles, which should be relaxing to assist in tone production, are now forcing and this causes the student to overblow. It is quite probable that these students are pushing the pitch above its tonal center.

Mouthpiece Pressure

Mouthpiece pressure is another of those problems which receives considerable discussion among trumpet players. Mouthpiece pressure has a significant relationship to tone quality. It should be understood that the often advocated no-pressure system of playing cannot possibly be achieved. There must be some seal where the mouthpiece contacts the lips. As one plays higher, the air velocity increases and unless *some* additional pressure is used, the air will escape from the point where the mouthpiece contacts the lips. If too much pressure is used, the tone has a forced quality, and the embouchure may be damaged. With too little pressure, the tone will have a weak, thin sound.

Many problems relating to excessive pressure can be traced to incorrect hand position. It is impossible to hold the instrument in the correct, relaxed manner, and use too much pressure. (See Chapter 2, "Hand Position and Playing Position.") If incorrect hand positions are causing excessive pressure, the corrections must begin here. Start by having the student relax the left hand grip on the instrument. Carefully observe the right hand position. If the little finger hook is being used to force the instrument against the lips, encourage the student not to use it. The hook may even be removed temporarily at a repair shop. Students with this problem should be restricted to playing in the middle register only until the arms can relax to the point where only the minimum mouthpiece pressure necessary is being used. The student may then gradually work into the upper register, being sure to rely on air velocity and embouchure muscles, rather than additional pressure.

The Double Oscillation

There is a unique aspect of mouthpiece pressure which puzzles many students and teachers. There are times when a student may play a note and have an audible distorted buzz of another pitch present in the tone. It sounds almost like a double stop on a stringed instrument except one note will be clear and the other distorted. (This should not be confused with the technique employed by some contemporary composers where one note is played while another is audibly sung.) It happens most often when the lip is quite fatigued. When this distortion occurs it is the fault of a second oscillation at the lip aperture. An uneven distribution of the weight of the mouthpiece on the top and bottom lips is the most frequent cause of this problem. Usually there is more pressure on the top lip than the bottom. The problem usually can be remedied by jutting the lower jaw forward slightly to equalize the pressure or by slightly changing the angle of the instrument. Occasionally it is necessary to increase the support from the muscles in the corners of the embouchure.

It should be understood that there is more than one acceptable example of good trumpet tone. Obviously, trumpeters in a symphony orchestra must have several tone concepts at their disposal. A professional would not use the same timbre on a Mahler symphony as he would on a Bach oratorio. The differences in tone quality in these cases depend on the key of the trumpet selected and the compatability of the mouthpiece. (These topics are discussed extensively in Chapter 8, "The Mouthpiece," Chapter 12, "The C Trumpet," and Chapter 13, "The Higher Key Trumpets.") These same concepts would apply to a soloist playing repertoire by various composers from various historical periods.

Similarly, commercial jazz players have a more brilliant tonal concept than players in a small combo. These performers will find that they can make the adjustment by choosing an instrument that has a bore, bell, and appropriate mouthpiece that will meet their playing demands.

Chapter 6
Articulation

The term articulation refers to the beginning and ending of musical notes and is not limited to those in which the tongue is utilized. Musical phrases are most often made up of a combination of slurred and tongued notes. Problems associated with slurring are discussed in Chapter 7, "Legato Playing," and this section will be devoted almost exclusively to those which use the tongue.

There are few areas in trumpet performance and teaching in which there are more diverse ideas than on the subject of articulation. The experienced teacher will be aware that this diversity of thought comes about because of the tremendous differences between individual players in regard to the size and shape of their tongues, teeth, palates, and jaws. This diversity makes it necessary to understand that no single, dogmatic idea will enable all students to articulate successfully.

On the other hand, there are many factors pertaining to articulation which are easy to define. It is easy for educated musicians to reach an agreement on the length of notes and the strength of the tongue.

This section will be devoted to these major areas of concern, together with common abuses associated with articulation. Incorrect use of the tongue is probably the most common problem facing trumpet students today.

The Tongue

The tongue is a large, mobile organ. When the mouth is closed the tongue occupies most of the oral cavity with the tip resting behind the top teeth and in contact with the hard palate at the front of the roof of the mouth.

There are three sections of the tongue which are related to trumpet playing. The tip is the most forward part of the tongue and is the part which has the most freedom of motion.

The top of the tongue is called the *dorsum* and though it is not able to move as freely as the tip, it may be raised and lowered in the oral cavity. The dorsum has a longitudinal membrane, the median raphé, which divides the area on each side into an arch.

The rear section of the dorsum is the *pharynegeal* section and represents the back third of the top of the tongue. Articulation using the pharyngeal section of the tongue is limited to double and triple tonguing.

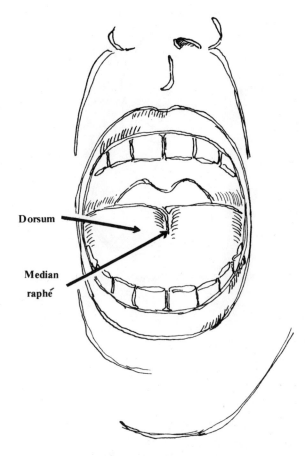

Dorsum

Median raphé

Fig. 37 Top of the Tongue

Its specific application is discussed in Chapter 17, "Multiple Tonguing."

The Function of the Tongue

The air passing through the embouchure aperture is sufficient to produce a musical tone. With practice, just blowing can be cultivated to produce a reasonable imitation of an articulation. The tongue has two basic functions in articulation. It acts as an air release valve and gives predictability to the moment when a note will respond. It also may be varied in strength and speed to match the appropriate loudness and character of the music. The player has a variety of ways to begin a note, just as a well-trained violinist has several ways to bow the strings.

not mean a performer has to use a combination of the two systems. Many players find that either type by itself is satisfactory for the complete range of articulation strengths and lengths.

Tongue Placement

Tip-tonguing

Tip-tonguing is the most commonly taught articulation technique. In fact, many teachers are not aware that any other type exists.

The tip of the tongue is placed behind the top teeth at the junction with the hard palate. The stroke of the tongue is downward and backward. When this occurs, air is released. A clean articulation is produced by pronouncing the syllable *Ta, Tu, Te,* or *Ti.* The strength of this articulation may be controlled by varying the speed of the tongue movement, the shape of the tip formation and the location of the tip as it touches on the back of the teeth.

Dorsal-tonguing

The tip of the tongue stays low in the mouth behind the bottom teeth when using dorsal-tonguing, and the dorsal surface of the tongue arches upward. As mentioned earlier in this section, there is a longitudinal membrane which forms a groove between the two arched halves of the tongue surface. The column of air is guided along this channel when the dorsal surface is removed from the hard palate. The most effective syllable to use for this articulation is *Da, Du, De,* or *Di.* The farther forward the dorsal surface is positioned on the flat palate, the more closely the dorsal-tonguing will resemble tip-tonguing.

I believe there are two main advantages to dorsal articulation. First, if the player uses an arched tongue when ascending into the upper register, the tongue is already positioned for high register articulation with the tip low in the mouth and the dorsum elevated toward the palate. Second, a wider variety of articulation strengths can be accomplished without having to change the basic dorsal placement.

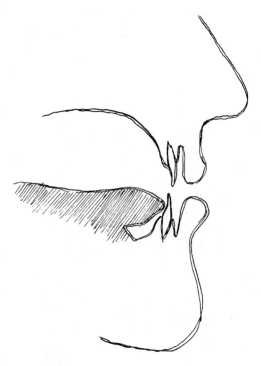

Fig. 38 Side of the Tongue—Flat Position

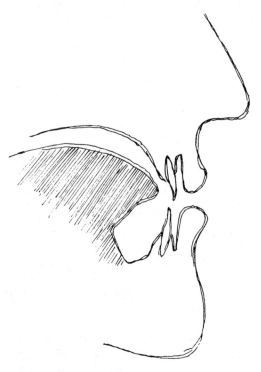

Fig. 39 Side of the Tongue—Arched Position

The tip-tonguing technique is most applicable to staccato articulation and dorsal-tonguing to legato articulation. It should be understood, however, this does

Normal Articulation

The articulation of any musical note represents a coordination of two functions—the stroke of the tongue and the duration of air. The stroke of the tongue is often called the attack. Using this word by itself is sometimes misleading because attack implies a certain amount of vigor or aggressiveness. It would be more correct to call this the release, because the tongue is acting as a valve to release the air to pass through the lips.

The following example represents the graphic shaping of a note using a normal articulation. There is no concern at this point regarding the length of the note.

The tongue provides the security of a definite beginning to the note without the feeling of an explosion. The strength of the articulation must be equal to the loudness of the note. If the articulation is too strong, there will be an unwanted accent; if it is too weak, the unmusical effect of sneaking into the notes will be created.

Terminating a note is similar to ending a note when singing—the flow of air is stopped, the throat remains open, and (assuming that more notes are to be performed on that breath) the support remains constant. Closing the glottis to stop the notes will create many negative results—the termination will be too abrupt, the throat will be tense, the tone will be restricted, and successive articulations will have an explosive quality because of the buildup of excess air in the throat.

Philip Farkas in *The Art of Brass Playing* describes every note as closing with a taper. This does not mean a gradual diminuendo is always necessary. In many cases the taper lasts only a fraction of a second, but

it gives a ring to the end of the note rather than an abrupt clip.

It is much more difficult for students to comprehend how a note should be ended than it is for them to understand the beginning. Poor releases, particularly those that are clipped, represent one of the most serious musical errors a student can commit and it is a difficult habit to change.

There are two major errors which students commonly make when terminating a note. The first is to release the note with the tongue closing off the airstream. This error is easily identified because the note will have an ending that is abrupt, clipped, or even accented. If the note is articulated *Ta,* tongue release would be represented as *at.*

The second fault is a release with an abrupt closing of the throat. Although the effect is not generally as unmusical as the tongue cutoff, the physical adjustments necessary are greater and correction takes more time. The throat release may be identified by a guttural sound (almost a grunt) emitted from the player's throat.

Similar techniques are used to correct each of these faults. The student should begin by playing half notes alternating with half rests. The note is sustained at a *mezzo forte* dynamic for the time equal to a dotted quarter note, and is then given a carefully tapered ending through the remaining value of the half note.

The student should be careful that the ending has an even taper with no abruptness. This exercise can be practiced with increasing speed as control is gained. The next step is to develop the taper when playing consecutive notes.

The most difficult problem to correct is the throat cutoff in the high register. This requires considerable patience and should be mastered in the middle and low register before attempting to play above the staff.

Note Lengths

In any given time value, musical notes have four basic lengths—*legato, portato, staccato,* and *staccatissimo. Legato* articulation is notated as follows:

A softer than normal articulation syllable is used for legato tonguing. The syllable *Da* is pronounced with the tongue in either the tip-tonguing or dorsal-tonguing position; however, the latter is easier for most players. The stroke of the tongue is somewhat slower than with a normal articulation. The maximum speed for repeti-

tions of the *legato* tongue is limited, but the characteristic style of *legato* music does not necessitate quickness. There is no release to the *legato* tongue when there are successive notes of the same style. One note leads directly into the next with the tongue interrupting the continuous airstream.

Portato articulation is notated as follows:

The tongue placement for the *portato* articulation is the same as the *legato* tongue. The *Da* syllable gives the note a satisfactory beginning. The basic difference occurs with the termination of the note. A small space is implied between the notes and this is produced by interrupting the airstream.

Some authors contend that the *portato* note should be played one-half of its written value but this rule is not universally true. The actual length may be determined by several factors including the tempo of the music, the style of the music and the conductor's interpretation.

Staccato articulation is notated as follows:

There is considerable disagreement about the length of *staccato* notes. Initially most students are taught that *staccato* means short. It is more correct to think of the note as being detached since the word short is quite subjective. Many people forget that *staccato* markings may be found on half notes as well as notes of smaller value. If short was the only goal, the *staccato* half note would be the same length as the *staccato* sixteenth note and there would be no reason to write notes of different lengths. As with the *portato* articulation, the style and tempo of the music and the interpretation of the conductor will be factors which determine how detached the *staccato* will be. There is, however, considerably more space with the *staccato* than with *portato* articulation.

Less of the tongue is used to produce the *staccato*.

If tip-tonguing is employed, the player can think of bringing the tip to more of a point against the back of the top teeth. If dorsal tonguing is used, the surface area of the tongue against the palate is smaller. The *staccato* tongue stroke is shorter and quicker. The note ends by terminating the air, not by closing the throat.

A special problem exists when articulating a long, continuous line of *staccato* notes at a fast tempo. In this case no ending is necessary for the individual notes. The notes are formed by a steady flow of air and rapid strokes of the tongue. This is not unlike the length of the *legato* tongue, but the small tongue surface and the rapid strokes give a lighter sound.

Any attempt to space the rapid notes will make the musical line sound choppy and the maximum tempo will be limited.

Staccatissimo articulation is notated as follows:

The *staccatissimo* is the most brief note duration. Tongue placement and speed are the same as with *staccato* tonguing. The division between *staccato* and *staccatissimo* is quite fine and mature musical judgment is required to determine which is appropriate. The *staccatissimo* is used infrequently and only when the character of the music justifies that style.

Accents

All of the previously mentioned types of articulation represent various tongue positions and note lengths. The common consideration for all of these notes is the fact that the musical dynamic remains the same throughout the note.

The same is not true with accents. Accents are played by using a more firm tongue stroke to give the beginning of the note more emphasis. A common fault when students play accents is that they always have the accent

loud and let the sustained part of the note drop down to a soft dynamic, as in the following example:

The correct interpretation of this would be:

Notice that the principal part of the note is played at the suggested musical dynamic. The accents are

superimposed on that dynamic with a firmer tongue stroke.

The *marcato* accent is indicated:

This is basically the same as the normal accent, but the tongue stroke is still stronger.

The heaviest accent is the *sforzando* (*sfz*) and is indicated:

This accent is well above the dynamic level of the music being played. The *rinforzando* (*rfz*) is quite similar to the *sforzando* but it has less definition to the beginning of the note. The *rinforzando* is actually like a quick

and strong crescendo and is executed more with the breath than the tongue.

The one accent which has a substantial dynamic change is the *forte-piano:*

It is essential to drop down to the level of *piano* immediately after the *forte* is played. In many cases, the change is made too slowly and gives the incorrect impression of a *diminuendo*. The *forte* is executed with a strong tongue stroke, though not as forceful as the *sforzando*. Sensitive breath control is necessary so that the sudden dynamic change does not disrupt the continuity of the air flow. Too little air and the lip will stop vibrating, too much air and the effect of the

dynamic change is lost.

Errors in Slurring

At the beginning of this chapter it was mentioned that approaching a note by a slur was as much a part of articulation as tonguing. It is important to note one of the most common slurring errors. When a combination of slurred notes is followed by one which is tongued, many students habitually lift the last note of the slur.

This error is made because students feel they need to prepare for the tongued note which follows. The lift does nothing but interrupt the smooth musical flow the passage should have. If the teacher encounters this problem, he would be wise to demonstrate simple combinations of slurred and tongued notes. The student should then repeat them after the teacher to try and duplicate the length of the release. Persistence and patience on the part of both the student and teacher, together with a discussion of the correct musical style, should correct the problem.

The lift to the last note would be incorporated only if the same passage were written:

When this effect is desired, the student should realize the detachment should be subtle, with no trace of abruptness.

Another common fault is to emphasize the tongued note at the beginning of a slurred passage.

This should be avoided unless there is some musical indication of an accent.

Conclusion

Teachers are expecting too much if they assume that young students will automatically make correct musical judgments regarding articulation styles. This knowledge comes with explanation, demonstration, and patience.

Once students become aware of the different articulation possibilities and can execute them correctly, they will welcome the opportunity to implement them. These articulation styles are some of the elements which can make a musical composition interesting and challenging. The teacher who neglects to show students more than the most basic types of articulation is omitting an important facet of music.

Chapter 7
Legato Playing

The correct approach to legato style on the trumpet and cornet demands both maturity and practice. Part of the difficulty in developing this approach is a result of the way most elementary method books begin the student with reading. Note the following example, which could be found in any one of several elementary method books.

Notice how the exercise focuses the student's concentration on only one note at a time. The note is articulated and released without any concern about what follows each single note.

Naturally, we must acknowledge the fact that the beginner is limited by an undeveloped breath control and an inability to hold the embouchure muscles steady. Most students are able to hold a beginning tone for four counts at a moderate tempo. The following exercise would provide a practical approach to the development of reading and musical continuity for the beginning student:

By using this approach we eliminate problems which might occur later. Comparison to a student who is learning to read may be helpful. While it is necessary to know each word to read a sentence, the sentence means nothing if those words are disjointed and fragmented.

Even at an early stage of development, a student can pick out familiar tunes "by ear" on the instrument. This process will help him to relate to the musical sentence and continuity of tone. For this reason, I feel it is advantageous to have a student work without a formal lesson book for at least the first few weeks of his training. In this way he has the opportunity to associate the instrument with what he already may be able to do instinctively.

The most important point to remember when trying to develop legato style and slurring is that the air flow must be continuous. Any interruption of the air stream causes a similar interruption in tone. This in turn breaks the musical sentence.

Lip Slurs

The term lip slurs applies to notes which change pitch without changing the valve combinations, but the name itself is not an accurate description of how these slurs are executed.

Upward Slurs

There are three basic physical changes which occur during the execution of upward lip slurs. First, the abdominal support of the air column is increased. Second, the muscles in the corners of the embouchure are firmed for additional support. Third, the tongue arches inside the mouth to increase the velocity of the air stream. To assist the tongue's upward movement, the student should think the syllable *ee*. One must be careful not to close the throat as the tongue arches. This constriction often distorts the tone.

If the tempo of the slur is quite slow, it is possible for the abdominal and embouchure changes to take place before the note change is actually desired, with the tongue arch coming just at the moment of change.

If the response of the upper note of the slur is hesitant, it can be assisted by adding an *H* to the tongue arch, and saying a *Hee* sound.

The *H* produces a small breath impulse and will help to overcome the added resistance of the upper note.

In addition to being careful that the throat does not close, the student must take care that the corners of the embouchure do not rise into a smiling position. Smiling can constrict the opening of the aperture, restrict the air passing through it and make the tone thin and pinched.

Most young students notice that they can move to the upper register fairly easily by either rolling the lower lip in, raising the jaw, or by a combination of both.

While this may provide some temporary success, it can be harmful over a period of time. Both of these actions tend to pinch the aperture closed so that the most resonant sound in the upper register cannot be achieved.

Downward Slurs

For downward lip slurs, a relaxation of muscles occurs. The tongue lowers in the mouth and the oral cavity is enlarged. The embouchure muscles become less firm, and the diaphragm support of the air column is reduced.

Lip Slur Errors

There are several common lip slur errors committed by students who have not fully developed control of the embouchure muscles, breath support, and tongue position. One of the most common faults is that the pitch of the first note of the slur will go sharp before an upward slur or go flat in anticipation of a downward slur. This problem comes about when the lip muscle adjustment is too slow. More often than not, when the second note of the slur actually comes, it will change too abruptly.

A second occurrence is that the tone will stop for a fraction of a second between the slurred notes. This is caused by a lack of control with the breath support.

This lack of control allows a temporary interruption of the air flow.

There are also three common mistakes related to the speed with which the embouchure muscles, breath support, and tongue position change. First, an intermediate note may be sounded between the two slurred pitches. Obviously this happens because all the necessary physical adjustments come too slowly. Second, an upward slur is missed by going too high or too low. Third, a downward slur is missed by going too high or too low. In both of the latter cases the teacher should determine if the problem is aural (the student does not have a mental image of the pitch he seeks) or physical (the adjustments are not coming quickly enough). The teacher should have the student tongue both notes to set the pitch impression in his mind. After the pitch change is secure, the slur can be added.

Changing Valve Combinations

In some respects, slurs are assisted by a change in the valve combination. As the valve is either depressed or raised, it breaks the air column inside the instrument. This break reduces the need for sensitive lip adjustments unless the slur is very wide.

It is important to keep in mind that regardless of the tempo of the selection being played, the fingers must move quickly and solidly. For this reason it is imperative that the right hand be in the correct playing position and relaxed.

A student generally will not have difficulty moving the fingers quickly in a fast tempo; however, the tendency in a slow passage is to make the valve changes slowly. A slow valve change creates an effect similar to a *glissando* on the trombone. Fragmented scales, such as the following exercises, played at a slow tempo, will aid in achieving definitive pitch changes.

Exercise played both legato-tongued and slurred
Play on all scale steps

It is important to keep in mind that at the slow tempo, the breath support and breath flow must remain constant. If it does not, the exercise will have a hard, pulsating line—almost as if the note were being played with breath accents.

Two of the best books for the development of a good legato style at various tempi are Herbert L. Clarke's *Technical Studies* (C. Fisher) and Robert Nagel's *Speed Studies* (Mentor Music). The main purpose of each of these books is the development of technical agility. Slow practice, with the valves being depressed solidly, will cultivate the fast, solid finger technique necessary for smooth, sustained playing.

Lip Flexibility Studies

Lip flexibility studies are basically lip slurs executed at a fast tempo to develop agility on the instrument. The following examples from Charles Colin's *Lip Flexibility Studies, Vol. I* illustrate the increasing demand for control of the air and lip as the exercises become more difficult.

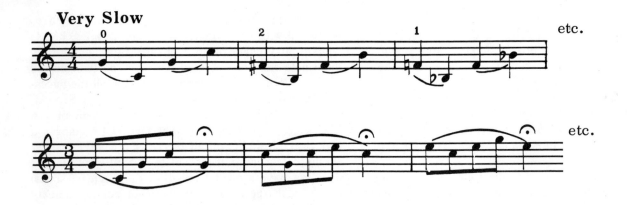

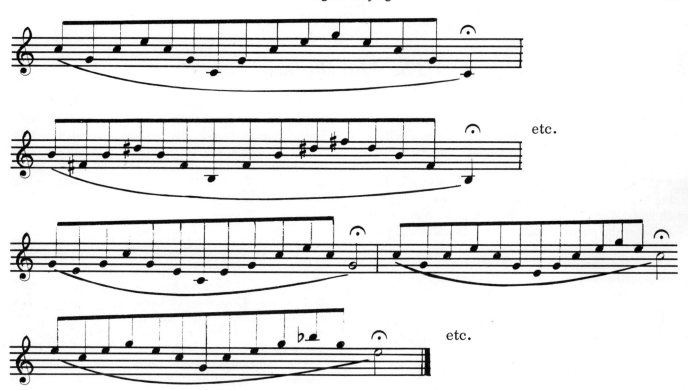

The student should keep in mind that extraneous embouchure motion on these exercises should be kept to a minimum. The common error of most students is to allow the corners of the embouchure and the chin to adjust for each note. Many students also feel that pivoting the head is necessary in flexibility studies. If excessive motion can be kept to a minimum, the overall tempo of the study can be increased and the end result will be smoother.

The one area where some motion may be necessary is in the extreme low register (between modes of vibration numbers two and three). In that range it is often necessary to drop the jaw slightly to get the necessary resonance to the tone. It should be kept in mind, however, that the corners of the embouchure should still retain some support or the tone will not maintain the proper center.

Flexibility studies should be practiced slowly at first until the proper feeling of embouchure muscle support, tongue position adjustment, and breath control is achieved.

When lip flexibility studies are approached and utilized correctly they not only develop fluency in slurring, but can be one of the main keys to expanding the upper register and building endurance.

Chapter 8
The Mouthpiece

The choice of a mouthpiece can be a critical factor in a trumpet player's success. In fact, the quality of mouthpiece is often more important than that of the instrument.

If you consider all the variables possible, there are literally thousands of mouthpieces from which to choose. When making a decision it is important to consider the player's degree of advancement, physical features, playing demands, and type of instrument. To add to the confusion each manufacturer has his own cataloguing system, with no uniform procedure between companies. One maker may use only a single letter or number to identify a specific mouthpiece, another may use as many as four. One may use higher numbers to identify large size mouthpieces, another smaller numbers for that size.

Therefore, it is important to obtain the catalogs of the various mouthpiece manufacturers to make an educated choice from the multitude of models. It is also advisable to seek advice from a specialist on the trumpet before making this critical decision.

The particular factors which are important in choosing a mouthpiece are: rim, cup, throat (sometimes separated to include throat shoulder or second cup), backbore and shank. All of these units must be balanced together to give a mouthpiece which has good overall playing characteristics.

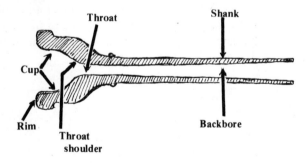

Fig. 40 The Mouthpiece

The Rim

One of the most obvious functions of the rim is for it to be shaped to provide maximum comfort for the player. Rims which are more rounded generally allow the player to have increased flexibility, but tend to reduce endurance. A flat rim provides a more definite termination point for the vibration of the lips, thus a sharper attack will be noticed. A flat rim may also add brilliance to the tone. A negative effect of the flat rim is that it tends to grip the embouchure and reduce flexibility.

The Cup

The two main considerations regarding the mouthpiece cup are the diameter and the depth. A combination of large diameter and depth allow for a cup volume which has the capacity to produce a full, resonant tone. Most players agree that an individual should use as large a mouthpiece as possible without going so far as to jeopardize comfort and control.

The larger cup diameter allows additional vibrating lip surfaces inside and also amplifies the volume of tone. A deeper cup allows the player to produce a fuller, more resonant timbre.

Playing a mouthpiece with a larger cup requires greater control of the embouchure muscles. There may be a temporary loss of security in the upper register when changing to the larger mouthpiece, but significantly more freedom of tone production will be noticed after a short period of adjustment.

Moving to larger size mouthpieces does not have to be done by gradual steps. When the student and teacher have decided on what they think will be a satisfactory choice, the change is made to that specific mouthpiece.

The Throat Shoulder (Second Cup) and Orifice (Throat)

The orifice of the mouthpiece is its narrowest portion. It is the cylindrical passage between the throat shoulder and the backbore. A mouthpiece that has an orifice which is too small will restrict the tone, particularly in the upper register. It also tends to "compress" the range of the instrument—the high notes become quite flat and the low notes quite sharp.

A large orifice, while producing a full, resonant tone, can also cause some problems. If the opening becomes too big it can be difficult to produce a controlled *pianissimo* dynamic. A large orifice also places greater physical demands on the embouchure of the performer.

The length of the orifice is also an important factor. A long orifice increases the resistance of the mouthpiece. It also tends to have the same compression effect on the intonation as the small orifice, the upper register notes are flatted and the lower register is sharped.

Manufacturers are becoming more aware that the shoulder of the throat (the bottom of the cup where it enters the orifice) is significant in the function of the mouthpiece. The particular shoulder primarily influences the tone quality and to some degree the resistance. A rounded throat shoulder will produce a more resonant tone than a comparable cup with a sharp throat shoulder.

The Backbore

The mouthpiece backbore has an influence on both intonation and tone quality. A mouthpiece in which the backbore is too small will have a stuffy, generally flat, upper register. Small backbores also tend to give a very brilliant tone quality.

A backbore which is too open will not have adequate resistance and the instrument will seem to respond with notes that lack definition or center. The tone will be too mellow and the player probably will find that the embouchure tires quickly.

The Shank

All instruments made in America have a mouthpiece receiver which is shaped with a Morse taper No. 1 (.050 inch per inch of length). The mouthpiece shank is made with this same taper. It is of utmost importance to have the end of the mouthpiece precisely meet the end of the mouthpipe inside the receiver. If the mouthpiece is too long or the receiver too short, the

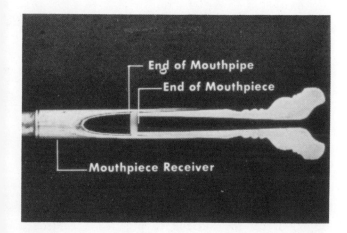

Fig. 41 Mouthpiece Fit in Receiver (*Courtesy of Schilke Music Products, Inc.*)

mouthpiece will not fit securely. If the reverse is true, or if the mouthpiece shank is too large, there will be a gap between the end of the mouthpiece and the end of the mouthpipe. This gap can cause serious problems by breaking the smooth surface on which the sound waves travel.

Dirt

The preceding points illustrate the critical dimensions of the mouthpiece. It goes without saying that if dirt is allowed to collect in the orifice or backbore of even a fine quality mouthpiece, this can greatly alter its playing characteristics. The mouthpiece should be cleaned thoroughly with a mouthpiece brush and soapy water at least once a week. Many players prefer to do this daily. (See photo in Chapter 27, "Fundamental Repair.")

Plating

Most mouthpieces are coated with silver plating, and when this becomes worn, the mouthpiece can be replated by the manufacturer or a competent repair shop with the proper facilities. If the plating becomes badly worn and the brass is exposed it may cause cold sores and fever blisters.

Some players prefer to use a gold-plated mouthpiece. They contend this makes the mouthpiece have a somewhat softer, warmer feel. It is not necessary to purchase a second mouthpiece of the same size to have one gold plated. It is possible to gold plate over an already existing silver finish.

Lucite or Plastic Mouthpieces

Mouthpieces may be made from lucite or plastic. These are particularly suited to outdoor playing in cold weather. For the most part, these mouthpieces are of marginal quality and should be used only when the temperature makes it impractical for a performer to use his regular mouthpiece.

Changing Mouthpieces for Different Instruments

The use of trumpets pitched in keys other than B-flat is discussed in Chapter 13, "The Higher-Key Trumpets." However, it should be mentioned here that most performers can switch mouthpieces to fit the playing properties of other trumpets without serious consequences.

I have found the same to be true with performers who play high parts in jazz bands and also do concert work requiring a different tone. If the individual fully understands the playing properties of his equipment, he can readily adapt to necessary changes.

Mouthpieces for the Beginner

With all the variables available in mouthpieces, it is understandable that the young student may become confused when trying to find the one best suited to his needs. There are two mouthpieces which are particularly tailored to the young player—the Bach 7C, and the Schilke 11. Both of these are available with either a trumpet or cornet shank. They both possess average playing characteristics, have the correct balance of dimensions and are consistently uniform in construction.

The beginning student would be well advised to consider buying one of these to improve the playing quality of the student line instrument. It is also important to remember that although varing brands of mouthpieces may look alike, they may produce significantly different results.

Chapter 9
Instrument Variables

The wide varieties of playing styles and professional demands have created a need for instruments which will allow trumpeters a broad range of choice. We are fortunate to have manufacturers who are willing to spend large sums of money on research and development to refine existing instruments and to create new models. Naturally, with trumpet being one of the most popular wind instruments, manufacturers recognize there is the possibility of a large customer market. It is to the mutual benefit of the makers and players to have a wide selection of instruments. Examining some of the common variables in trumpets and cornets will give some insight into how the instrument may be matched to the player and his needs.

The Bore

The bore of the instrument is measured at the cylindrical valve section and is related to the instrument's freedom of blowing or resistance. Trumpets in the larger bore sizes have a more resonant tone quality. This, however, can have some disadvantages. Students will need to consciously put more air into the instrument to realize its full potential. Players with weak embouchures find a large instrument can decrease their endurance.

The trend in recent years has been an increase in bore size. Most students with correct embouchures and good playing habits will find that a medium-large bore (.458 inch–.461 inch) instrument matches their playing capability. Instruments can also be found with medium bore (.452 inch–.457 inch) and large bore (.462 inch–.468 inch). The medium bore instrument requires slightly less air and might be selected by a student of small physical stature. The large bore trumpet would be reserved for the player with a rigorous embouchure and who prefers an instrument which is free blowing.

The Bell

The function of the bell is to act as a radiator and resonator of the vibrations in the instrument. Three factors are important in bell construction: the formula of the metal, the rate of expansion of the conical bore section and the overall diameter of the end of the bell.

All brass is an alloy of copper and zinc, although it also contains minor traces of other metals. For general purposes the amount of copper may constitute between 55 and 95 percent of the total formula. The common figure used in trumpet construction is about 70 percent. This is known as yellow, or high brass. When the copper content of the formula is raised to 80–85 percent it is called red, or low brass. The higher copper content makes the metal softer, giving a somewhat more resonant tone quality. This additional resonance might be preferred by players who have a brilliant tone as it would tend to make it easier for them to blend into a section.

The area of the bell where the trade mark is found on most trumpets is called the throat or flair. A larger throat increases the resonance of the bell, but one should be careful not to select a throat that is too large. If the throat is too large the trumpet sound will not have adequate projection.

The diameter of the end of the bell is the least critical of the three factors. The size is generally related to the bore of the instrument and the resonating qualities desired. A medium-large or large bore instrument will usually have a bell 4-3/4 inches to 5 inches in diameter. A medium bore will be 4-1/2 inches to 4-3/4 inches.

Tuning Slide and Water Key

The tuning slide and water key are two seemingly insignificant factors that cause concern among performers who seek to have their instrument play with optimum uniformity and refinement.

If it is necessary to pull out the tuning slide excessively to have the correct pitch when playing in an ensemble or with a piano, it will distort the evenness of bore in two places. (See Fig. 42)

A gap will be created at the top and the bottom of the slide. One prominent manufacturer, Renold Schilke, has gone so far as to eliminate the tuning slide altogether on certain models of his instruments. Tuning is accomplished by lengthening the bell with a slide and set screw arrangement. A gap at this point is significantly less critical. (See Fig. 43)

A player who has to pull out his tuning slide excessively may also wish to consider having a longer leadpipe installed. However, before this is attempted, it should be determined that the embouchure muscles are functioning correctly. Pinching the aperture will cause the

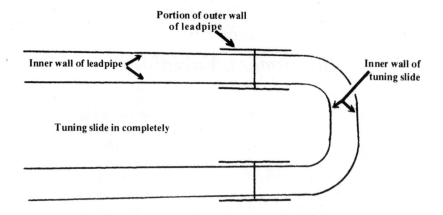

Portion of outer wall
of leadpipe

Inner wall of leadpipe

Inner wall of
tuning slide

Tuning slide in completely

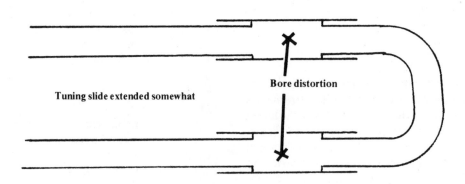

Tuning slide extended somewhat

Bore distortion

Fig. 42 Space in Inner Bore Caused by Extending the Tuning Slide

Fig. 43 Adjustable Tuning Bell—Detail (see also Figs. 50, 51, and 52)

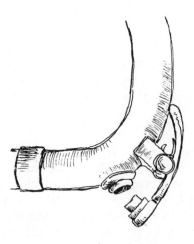

Fig. 44 Water Key Cork with Nipple

pitch to be sharp. In this case an adjustment of the instrument should not become a substitute for correct playing habits.

When a critical point of the vibrating air column (nodal point) falls at the water key, the blowing characteristics of the instrument may be changed slightly. Some performers who are bothered by this will have an instrument repair shop remove the water key and cover the hole. If this is done the player must pull the slide and drain the water as is common with the French horn. In time this can become a tedious task.

Two alternatives to removing the water key might be to turn the tuning slide upside down to avoid the nodal point, or to use a water key cork with a nipple which extends up into the water key recess. This fills the hole for the most part. (See Fig. 44)

The player could also consider the Amado water key as used on the Getzen instruments. This is constructed in a piston-sleeve arrangement so the recess is closed when the water key is not being used. (See Fig. 45)

Most of the details in the description of these instrument variables will apply to only the most discerning trumpet performer. Indeed, less-experienced players may use the absence of these as excuses as to why they are not achieving satisfactory results. Thus such

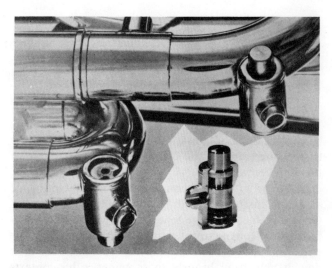

Fig. 45 Cross-Section of the Amado Water Key (*Used by permission of Ray Amato, inventor and the Getzen Company Incorporated, exclusive distributor.*)

details should be considered as applicable to the person who has the correct approach to playing the trumpet, but is looking for perfection of every aspect of his playing.

Chapter 10
Trumpet / Cornet Differences

The concept of performance on musical instruments has been a thing of constant change. This is particularly true of the trumpet and cornet since the beginning of the 20th century.

In the early 1900's the cornet was a dominant influence as a solo instrument with concert and military bands. Generally speaking, the tone quality was light to complement the agile tongues and swift fingers of the performers. These virtuoso players were giants of their day, having been brought to prominence by contests and concert appearances.

During the same period the trumpet adopted a very minor role. Most of its critics felt the instrument was not capable of producing anything other than a brilliant, often harsh, tone. It began to assume some degree of prominence with the advent of jazz, although many of the early jazz players used cornets.

Today the roles of the cornet and trumpet are almost reversed. The cornet suffered a decline in popularity in the late 1930's and now the trumpet is by far the more popular instrument. If the trumpet was an instrument noted for its harshness at the turn of the century, the same cannot be said of it today. Its tone can range from bold to subdued, from brilliant to lyrical. The trumpet may be used in an unlimited number of ways which range from solo performance to ensemble playing, from jazz bands to symphony orchestras.

The trend in bands in the last 25 years has been toward the concept of duplicating the sound of an orchestral wind section. It was only natural that the trumpet would flourish under these conditions. It also was assumed that students who had professional performing aspirations in mind would take up the trumpet. With trumpet they could pursue a career in either the symphonic or dance band field. The cornet does not lend itself to this choice. The cornet player finds himself in much the same situation as a student who plays the euphonium. The euphoniumists discover that it becomes necessary for them to play the trombone also if they expect to find work professionally as performers. This does not mean that they have to sacrifice the instrument altogether, but the employment possibilities on the euphonium definitely are more limited.

Experiments conducted by the C. G. Conn Company have shown that in the hands of a skilled performer, it is very difficult to tell whether that person is playing a cornet or trumpet. There are, however, factors which make a significant difference between the two instruments and it is important that we examine the characteristics which make each of these instruments unique.

The first consideration is the mouthpiece. The cornet mouthpiece has the same taper to the shank as the trumpet mouthpiece, but the overall shank size is smaller. A cornet and a trumpet mouthpiece made by the same manufacturer with the same catalog number will have exactly the same dimensions in respect to rim shape and width, cup size, throat shoulder, and orifice. Only the shank is smaller.

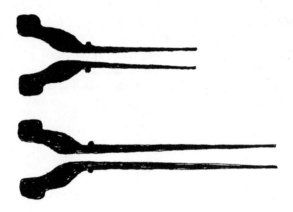

Fig. 46 Cornet (top) and Trumpet (bottom) Mouthpieces

The *true* cornet mouthpiece used when the instrument was in vogue had more of a funnel shape than the cup shape used today. The mouthpiece cup dimensions used by players today are so similar to those of trumpet cups that the two could be considered exactly alike.

The smaller mouthpiece shank size is a contributing factor to what is probably the major difference between the instruments. As the mouthpiece receiver is smaller, the manufacturer can build the instrument with almost a continuous conical bore. The cornet has conical bore for anywhere from 65 per cent to 90 per cent of its total length. The remainder is, of course, cylindrical. There can be no specific percentage as this is determined by the designer.

The trumpet has a cylindrical bore for 50 per cent to 65 per cent of its length. Not only is the percentage of conical bore in the trumpet less than the cornet, but because the mouthpiece shank is larger, the conical bore taper is more gradual.

Many people have the impression that the cornet is shorter than the trumpet. Actually this could not be true or the instruments would not be in the same key. They are exactly the same overall length.

Fig. 47 Cornet (right) and Trumpet (left)

The cornet, however, has two or three (depending on the manufacturer) 180 degree bends in its tubing before entering the valves, compared to one on the trumpet. This gives the cornet the appearance of being shorter. At least one manufacturer feels the double bend gives the instrument more resistance, making slurring on the cornet somewhat easier. Others may argue that the increased facility is because of the predominance of conical bore. Regardless, there is agreement by all that flexibility is easier on the cornet. More resistance, easier slurring and increased flexibility can be particularly important to the beginning student and this is the reason many band directors favor starting their students on cornets. There also is agreement that the beginner usually gets a good tone quality earlier

with the cornet. Many teachers feel that instilling this concept initially with the cornet will help students later if they switch to the trumpet.

Band directors may find themselves somewhat confused in choosing a particular player for a specific part as there are so many different ways composers and arrangers will divide cornet and trumpet parts. The most common divisions are three cornet parts combined with two trumpet parts, three trumpet parts alone or four trumpet parts alone. In the first combination, common in the marches of Sousa, Fillmore, *et al.,* and the band transcriptions made at the turn of the century (*e.g.* Chappell Band Library), the cornet parts are technically more demanding with the trumpets acting as reinforcements. In a case such as this, a director should use the more capable players on the cornet parts regardless of which instrument they are using.

The trumpet is the commonly specified instrument in orchestral scores. When the cornet is designated, orchestral music is usually scored for two trumpets and two cornets. For many years no distinction was made and all four parts were played on trumpets. Recently, however, many conductors have become more adamant about having cornets actually used to play those parts. This is particularly true in some of the major American orchestras which employ four full-time trumpet players. In smaller orchestras which have only two trumpet players the parts should be analyzed to see which parts are most necessary. In almost all cases this will be the two cornet parts. The two players should see to it that the most prominent pair of parts are covered first. After this is assured, it may be possible for the same two players to fill in some of the alternate pair of parts during measures rest.

It would be foolish to assume that the cornet is an instrument of the past even though its popularity has diminished to some degree. Its use today in the United States can be seen somewhat in a geographical association. This influence has been fostered by the fact that some fine college bands use the cornet extensively and individuals trained in these institutions help perpetuate its esteem. A few soloists also use the cornet in concert appearances, but often for historical rather than innovative interest. Contemporary composers seldom write for it. However, one notable exception is Stravinsky's *L'Histoire du Soldat* (1918) in which the cornet is specified and its tone color is intended.

Chapter 11
The Flugelhorn

Before the invention and application of valves, brass instruments were used primarily as signaling devices. This includes one of the lesser known members of the brass family, the flugelhorn. The name is derived from the word *flugeln,* meaning game trails. We can assume that it played a role in the hunt to signal the approach or presence of game.

It is presumed that valves were adapted to the instrument by Adolph Sax around 1840. He created a whole family of Saxhorns ranging from a soprano model in high E flat down through a contrabass in BB flat. The instrument which has survived in its nearly original concept is the mezzo-soprano model in B flat. Although Saxhorns are not presently built by any instrument manufacturer in the United States, the flugelhorn is similar to Saxhorns presently being built in Europe. The nomenclature tends to become confused because there are often substantial differences in construction between flugelhorns of various makers with some being more close to the Saxhorn concept than others.

Present-day flugelhorns have a valve bore size of approximately .459 inch. The mouthpiece receiver is the same size as a cornet and the instrument is nearly all conical bore. The rate of expansion of the bore, however, is much greater than the cornet, so much so that the throat of the bell is often more than double the diameter of the cornet. The overall diameter of the bell may be an inch or more larger than either the cornet or trumpet.

It is imperative that a suitable mouthpiece be used when playing the flugelhorn. Typically, the mouthpiece would have no cup shape at the bottom, and the inner walls would enter directly into the orifice. The cup has a basic funnel shape similar to the French horn mouthpiece. Trumpet and cornet players would find it possible to use a mouthpiece that has the same rim size as their normal mouthpiece.

The combination of the *V-shaped* mouthpiece and the rapidly expanding bore give the flugelhorn its subtle, mellow quality. The basic tone quality does not project well, so when it is used in combination with several other instruments its sonorous tone becomes a filler. Such is the case in brass ensembles when its tone quality is used to bridge the timbre between the clear, penetrating trumpets and the French horns.

In band scoring it is used to homogenize the tone of the brass and reed sections. They are usually scored as a pair of instruments and the parts are technically less demanding than the cornet and trumpet parts. Since it is quite common to have the range restricted to the staff and below, a director would be safe in assigning these parts to one of the less-advanced players, although the student should be thoroughly familiar with the playing problems of the flugelhorn.

There are a few examples of the flugelhorn used in orchestral writing, notably Ralph Vaughan Williams, *Symphony No. 9,* Heitor Villa-Lobos, *Three Movements for Wind Orchestra,* and *Threni* by Igor Stravinsky.

In recent years the flugelhorn has flourished in the jazz field. It has become a respected instrument in the hands of Clark Terry, Miles Davis, and Chuck Mangione. Some jazz emsembles will use the instrument with four or five players performing ballad melodies in unison. Having several flugelhorn performers play in unison is not easily accomplished, though it is highly effective when done well. Use only skilled musicians to achieve uniformity in balance, quality, and intonation.

The most practical range of the flugelhorn is from

Fig. 48 Flugelhorn

the lowest note, F sharp to the top notes of the treble staff. The flugelhorn's abundance of rapidly expanding conical bore makes it difficult to center the tone on notes above the staff.

In recent years some manufacturers have added a fourth valve to their flugelhorns. This extra valve is in F, producing the same note as the combination 1-3. The main advantage in having this extra tubing is that the range of the instrument can be lowered by five additional half steps, and as we have already noted, the area in the staff and below is the flugelhorn's strongest register. The fourth valve also may be implemented to assist with correction of notes which are somewhat out of tune with their conventional fingerings. These intonation deficiencies are examined in detail in Chapter 18, "Intonation Adjustments." The problems with flugelhorn intonation are similar to those on the trumpet and cornet as pointed out in that chapter. If the 1-3 combination is sharp on the flugelhorn, the fourth valve may be used by itself with the slide adjusted for optimum tuning of that pitch. In all probability this would also improve the tuning of the normally sharp 1-2-3 combination by making the substitution 2-4. The fingering chart below is suggested for use with most four-valve flugelhorns. It should be understood that this may vary to some extent with different instruments.

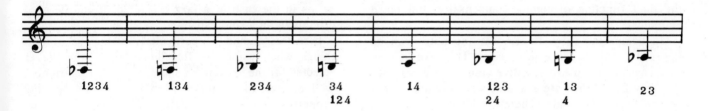

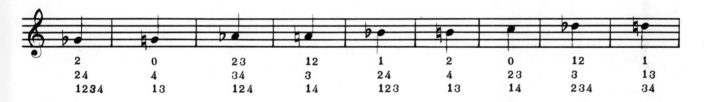

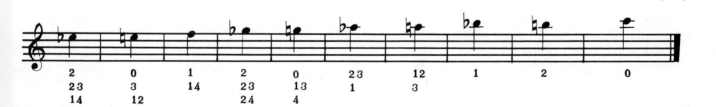

The tuning relationships of the fourth valve on the flugelhorn should be carefully examined. The length of the fourth valve slide is in relation to the other three valve slides. On some instruments each of the descending chromatic fingering combinations becomes progressively more sharp. By the time the player reaches the combination 1-2-3-4, he has not lowered the instrument by the five half steps one might expect, but the sharp pitches have caused the interval to diminish to only four half steps. This is the same principal by which the slide positions on the trombone become farther apart as one plays chromatically downward. More tubing must be added as the fundamental is lowered. The fourth valve slide length must then be a compromise to serve the dual function of tuning compensator and range extender.

On some four-valve flugelhorns the notes can be lowered by embouchure adjustment. This takes a keen awareness of pitch and sensitive embouchure control.

A few flugelhorns are available with a tuning trigger on the first valve slide. Thumb saddles and rings on the slides for intonation are uncommon on the flugelhorn because most of these instruments are constructed with the valve slides in a vertical position, rather than horizontal as with the trumpet and the cornet.

Many players prefer the three-valve flugelhorn to the four-valve instrument because they feel the extra valve makes the instrument more difficult to blow. You must remember that it is necessary to blow through the extra tubing connecting the valves and through the valve itself, even if the valve is not lowered to engage the additional tubing it controls.

Conclusion

The flugelhorn can be a valuable addition to the instrumentation of concert bands, stage bands, and brass ensembles. Its presence will add sonority to a section or, as in the case of a jazz ensemble, it can be used effectively in a solo capacity.

Directors should be particularly conscious of two things when using the flugelhorn. First, the player selected for the instrument should know the instrument well enough to be totally familiar with its blowing properties and intonation deficiencies. Second, if used in conjunction with other instruments, the timbre is a filler sonority rather than a solo tone. The actual presence of the flugelhorn is unnoticed as an individual sound when used in conjunction with other instruments.

Chapter 12
The C Trumpet

The C trumpet has risen in popularity over the last 25 years and is now the commonly used instrument in most orchestral trumpet sections in the United States. This instrument was recognized in France long before it came into its own in this country. The C trumpet is not universally accepted and there still are countries where the B flat trumpet is used almost exclusively for all types of performance.

Fig. 49 B flat (left) and C (right) Trumpets

There are three main reasons for selecting the C trumpet in orchestral playing:

1. The characteristic tone quality is prefered.
2. The response is lighter and quicker.
3. The fingering may often be less intricate by switching to another key.

The tone quality of the C trumpet is more brilliant than the B flat. The amount of brilliance is determined by the bore size, the leadpipe taper, and the bell size. The final results determined by these factors are all comparable to those which occur with the B flat trumpet and are discussed in detail in Chapter 9, "Instrument Variables." Although the mouthpiece could further alter the sound, most players use the same mouthpiece on both their B flat and C trumpets. The added brilliance of the C trumpet can be very helpful to the orchestral performer who has to project his part with ease through a large string section.

Notes on the C trumpet respond with a lighter articulation than on the B flat. As the length of the C trumpet is somewhat shorter and the tubing bends are closer together, the instrument has more resistance. Overcoming the resistance requires additional breath support. Consequently, the breath support decreases the effort which the tongue needs to exert to make the notes respond.

I remember reading an article several years ago by a respected performer and teacher. He commented that after using the C trumpet exclusively for a few weeks he switched back to the B flat. His impression for the first few minutes was that it felt like "walking a tightrope while wearing rubber boots." Regardless of that opinion, most players find it is possible to alternate back and forth between the instruments with little difficulty. The C trumpet's ease of response can be particularly helpful when playing a very soft, controlled articulation.

I consider the ease with which certain fingering patterns can be executed last in importance when making the decision as to which instrument to use, although I know many artist players for whom that is the most important factor. The object in this case would be to take a difficult key, for instance E Major on the B flat trumpet, and play the same piece in D Major on the C trumpet. In this way many of the awkard 2-3 valve combinations are eliminated.

Some students have the mistaken idea that the C trumpet is a shortcut to becoming proficient at transposition. Nothing could be farther from the truth. In fact, there are many parts written for B flat trumpet which are transposed and played on the C trumpet because the performer elects to do this for one or more of the reasons given previously.

An individual unfamiliar with the C trumpet might ask at this point, "If the instrument has this many advantages, why is it not used universally?" First, there

45

is the matter of tone quality. The more brilliant sound is certainly not acceptable for all circumstances. It would be much more difficult to blend the tone of a large section of trumpets, such as our modern concert bands employ.

The main concern, however, is that the C trumpet has more intonation problems than the B flat. Highly skilled performers in a symphony orchestra section are infinitely more competent to deal with these idiosyn-cracies than students who are still concerned with embouchure function and technical development.

Below is a chart showing the common tuning irregularities on both the B flat and C trumpets. The arrows with the notes show intonation discrepancies. A single arrow indicates a small adjustment is necessary. The double arrows show notes which require greater adjustment.

B flat Trumpet

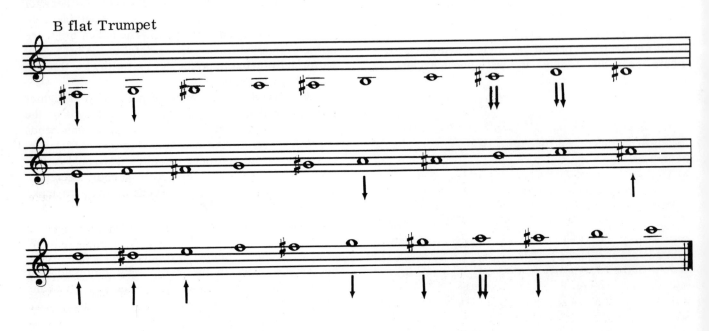

C Trumpet

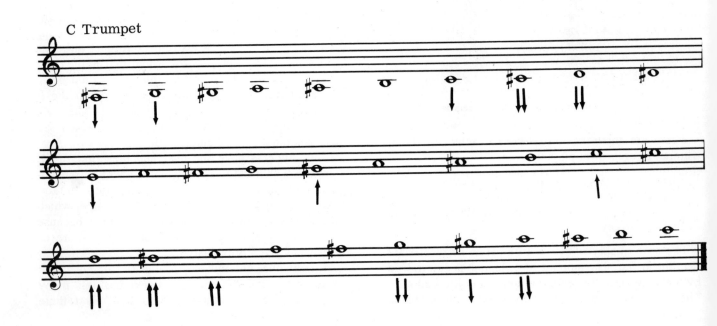

Tuning problems of moderate concern on the B flat trumpet are magnified on the C. These problems, of course, vary from one manufacturer to another and with different models of trumpets from the same maker. Intonation problems with most C trumpets are acute enough that it often becomes necessary to finger the fourth space E 1-2 instead of 0, and the fourth space E flat 2-3 instead of 2. A few players choose to play the A above the staff 3 instead of 1-2 and the third space C 2-3 instead of 0. It should be pointed out, however, that design improvements by some instrument makers in the last few years have made major improvements which help solve these tuning problems.

Choosing a C Trumpet

Assuming a player has developed a solid embouchure, technical proficiency, a good tone, and a mature concept of musical styles on the B flat trumpet, he may wish to buy a C trumpet. There are three basic sounds for which C trumpets are chosen.

Some players favor a tone similar to the B flat trumpet. An instrument which has a large mouthpipe bore (approximately .462 inch) combined with a bell having a large throat (the area approximately 4 inches from the end of the bell where the trademark is usually found) and an end diameter of 4-7/8 to 5 inches will produce a timbre which is not too brilliant. This type of trumpet would be preferred by players in large orchestras when they do not wish to have a tone with the brilliance usually associated with the C trumpet. In the last few years some orchestras in the United States, namely the Chicago Symphony and the Minnesota Orchestra, have purchased European rotary-valve C trumpets for their entire trumpet sections. These trumpets are used on some works by German composers from the Romantic Period, such as Brahms and Bruckner.

At the other end of the spectrum is what is commonly known as the *French* C trumpet. The bell has a much more narrow throat, a smaller overall diameter (approximately 4-3/4 inches) at the end, and probably a somewhat smaller (.458 inch) mouthpipe bore size. This trumpet would be suitable for performing solo literature by French composers, in chamber ensembles, or with small orchestras. The characteristics of the French C trumpet are a very brilliant tone at loud dynamics and easy response.

A compromise between these two is a C trumpet with a moderate size bell, using a smaller throat than the B flat but the same overall bell diameter (4-7/8 inches). Either a medium-large (.458 inch) or large bore (.460 inch) mouthpipe is used with this instrument so that the trumpet still has the inherent tone and playing qualities of the C trumpet. This is the most universally used C trumpet because it is adaptable for all types of playing—from solo literature though large symphony orchestras.

An individual should assess his playing demands and, after careful consideration, look for the instrument which has the tone most practical for his needs. After this has been determined, the player can try various brands of instrument having models that fit into these general specifications.

It is helpful to have a Stroboconn or some other mechanical means available to check intonation deficiencies. For the person who has not played a C trumpet very much, there may be a problem when he tries to check the intonation by himself. If a proper technique is not used or a proper tone produced, the intonation produced may be worse than the trumpet normally has. For that reason, have a professional performer who is familiar with C trumpets play several instruments to help make the choice. An experienced player would know what intonation problems should eliminate an instrument from consideration and what is within a tolerable limit.

Adapting to the Instrument

When becoming familiar with the C trumpet, it is important to keep in mind the tone quality of the instrument. Becoming overly concerned with the additional brilliance of the tone may cause embouchure adjustments which will not only impair progress on that instrument, but prove detrimental to overall playing. The player must strive for a C trumpet sound, not the familiar B flat sound. Begin by playing long tones and later work into scale patterns for refinement of intonation.

It is important that the student play the C trumpet for a while every day during his first contact with the instrument. Every time the instrument is approached, care must be taken to anticipate the unique properties and qualities of the instrument.

In my own teaching, I assign enough material so I know that advanced students who play the C trumpet will be spending about half of their practice time on the C trumpet. This material need not be limited to solos and orchestral excerpts. Basic technical material, etudes, transposition studies, and phrasing studies also should be included.

The C Cornet

I vividly recall attending a trumpet clinic in the mid-1950s given by the late Vincent Bach. He did all his performing on a C cornet and expressed the opinion that this was his favorite instrument because of its blowing ease and beautiful tone.

There is evidence that the C cornet was used in symphony orchestras during the late 19th century. As the popularity of concert bands increased, the B flat cornet assumed the role in those ensembles. The C cornet then was relegated to performers who used it to play solo lines written in concert pitch from piano scores, somewhat like a C melody saxophone.

Two notable figures who occasionally use the C cornet in their orchestral performing at the present time are Armando Ghitalla, Principal Trumpet of the Boston Symphony, and Frank Kadarabek, Principal Trumpet of the Philadelphia Orchestra.

Conclusion

In the last 30 years the C trumpet has risen from a position of obscurity to the instrument commonly used by symphony orchestra trumpeters today. It is also frequently used in solo performances and chamber music. Obviously any serious trumpet student will find it essential to become adept on the C trumpet, but only after achieving security in all the basic elements of B flat trumpet playing.

Chapter 13
The Higher-Key Trumpets

The D-E flat Trumpet

The D trumpet is used less frequently than it was before the major technological improvements in the piccolo A-B flat instrument. Formerly it was assumed the D trumpet parts in the cantatas and oratorios of J. S. Bach should be played on the modern D instrument even though they were originally played on a natural trumpet pitched an octave lower. These parts are now appreciably easier on the piccolo trumpet.

The D and E flat trumpets are often built as one instrument with separate tuning slides for each key. In the case of the Schilke D-E flat, there are separate bells for each key. The proximity of the two keys makes the instrument compatible without needing to have two sets of valve slides.

These trumpets will play satisfactorily with the same mouthpiece as used on the B flat or C trumpet; however, they are often played with a somewhat smaller mouthpiece. The smaller mouthpiece helps to give the instrument what is recognized as its characteristic tone quality.

There are three basic bore and bell combinations with the D-E flat trumpets: The smallest of these has a small (.401 inch) bore and a small bell. The next size larger has a medium (.450 inch) bore and a medium bell. Either of these is well suited to the high trumpet parts of Bach since the tone is clear and centered. These instruments are not so large as to overpower a solo vocalist or choir.

The third D-E flat trumpet is a combination of medium large (.458 inch) bore and medium bell. This instrument has a tone quality which is more resonant and is well suited for playing the Haydn and Hummel concertos. For players who wish to perform the Hummel *Concerto* in the original key of E major, a replaceable E bell is available for the Schilke F-G trumpet mentioned later in this chapter. Original experiments with adding the E bell to the D-E flat body showed that the tuning was inferior to the E bell and the F-G trumpet body.

There is a fourth type of D trumpet which is not interchangable with E flat. That is a large (.459 inch) bore instrument with a bell approximating that of a C trumpet. This oversized D instrument is useful to players who elect to play orchestral passages in that key because of the ease of fingering, but want to duplicate the full bodied tone of a C trumpet.

The D-E flat trumpets have tuning problems on notes similar to the C trumpet, but they are more pronounced. As I have mentioned before, the player should be acutely aware of these deficiencies so that alternate fingerings or slide adjustments can be utilized where necessary. (See Chapter 12, "The C Trumpet.")

In recent years Schilke has added an optional fourth valve to its tuning bell D-E flat and F-G trumpets. This fourth valve lowers the fundamental note a perfect fourth. It may be used in the same manner as a compensator to correct some tuning deficiencies. When the instrument is in E flat the fourth valve is particularly useful. With a fourth valve, the range of the E flat instrument has the same compass as the *mezzo-soprano* B flat trumpet. (Mezzo-soprano is the name given to the commonly known B flat trumpet to avoid confusion with the piccolo B flat, or *sopranino,* trumpet.) This is especially useful on Franz Joseph Haydn's *Concerto in E flat.* The low register has the fullness available from the B flat instrument, while the high register has the delicacy of an E flat.

Fig. 50 D Trumpets—Small Bore (left), Tuning Bell (center), and Large Bore/Long Bell (right)

Fig. 51 Tuning Bell Trumpet—Detail (see also Fig. 43)

Some players prefer to perform the following passages from the orchestral literature on the D or E flat trumpet. Naturally, this selection is entirely a matter of personal taste.

Bartok, B. *Concerto for Orchestra*—final movement (E flat)

Kodaly, Z. *Hary Janos*—cornet part in the fifth movement (E flat)

Mahler, G. *Symphony No. 3*—posthorn solo (D)

Prokofiev, S. *Lieutenant Kije*—off-stage solo (D)

Ravel, M. *Alborada del Gracioso*—(D)

Ravel, M. *Piano Concerto*—(D)

Respighi, O. *Pines of Rome*—off-stage solo (D)

Rimsky-Korsakoff, N. *Russian Easter Overture* (D)

Stravinsky, I. "Danse Infernale" from *The Firebird*—(D)

Stravinsky, I. *Pulcinella*—(D)

Tschaikovsky, P. *Capriccio Italien*—solo (E flat)

Tschaikovsky, P. *Symphony No. 4*—opening (E flat)

Tschaikovsky, P. "Le Chocolat" from *The Nutcracker* (E flat)

Wagner, R. *Parsifal*—prelude (E flat)

The F-G Trumpet

The F-G trumpet is used less often than the D-E flat; however, its availability is worth mentioning. Like

the D-E flat, the F-G trumpet has become less useful as the improved piccolo A-B flat (discussed later in this chapter) is being more commonly used. As the difference in pitch between the F and G trumpets is a full step, it is necessary to have both a tuning slide or tuning bell *and* three additional valve slides.

Fig. 52 F-G Trumpet (tuning bell F trumpet with interchangeable G bell at right)

The F-G trumpet, like the D-E flat, also is available from some manufacturers with a fourth valve. This serves the same function as a range extender and tuning compensator.

The F-G trumpet is commonly found with a small (.401 inch) bore and small bell. The tone is similar to the small D trumpet designed for oratorio playing. A smaller mouthpiece must be used with the F-G trumpet to produce the proper tone quality.

The F-G trumpet is most frequently used on the *clarino* parts of J. S. Bach, and a player might elect to use this trumpet if he desired a more resonant tone than could be produced on the piccolo A-B flat. With the larger tone of the F-G trumpet, a second trumpet player might use it to achieve a more balanced sound in a section of three trumpets playing a work by Bach. It would be perfectly acceptable to play the following excerpt with the first player using a piccolo A trumpet, the second playing a G trumpet, and the third playing a D trumpet. The overall sound would be more balanced than if the same passage were played with trumpets one and two using piccolos and a D trumpet on the third part.

as written

in D

It is also possible to have a fouth valve on the F-G trumpet. Its function is the same as on the D-E flat, as a tuning compensator and range extender. Lowering the instrument a perfect fourth is particularly helpful when playing D parts on the G instrument. The player has the full range compass of the D trumpet as well as the assistance of the G trumpet in the high register.

The Piccolo A-B flat Trumpet

Technological improvements in the piccolo A-B flat trumpet in recent years have made this instrument more practical to use in a wide variety of circumstances. It can be heard on everything from J. S. Bach's *Brandenburg Concerto No. 2* to commercial jingles on television.

Many students have the misconception that switching from a *mezzo-soprano* B flat trumpet to a piccolo B flat will automatically give them unlimited additional range. Nothing could be further from the truth. A piccolo

trumpet may help them produce two or three notes higher than the top of their range on a *mezzo-soprano* instrument, but is in no way a solution to instant upper register. An extra octave cannot be bought with money. The main reason for choosing the piccolo trumpet is that the notes in its high register have much more definition to them. This eliminates the precarious sliding around between pitches which would occur with the lower instrument.

The mouthpiece used with the piccolo trumpet has a more shallow cup and smaller diameter rim than that which is used with the *mezzo-soprano* instruments. Most performers experience no difficulty in switching between a mouthpiece compatible with the piccolo trumpet and their B flat trumpet mouthpiece. The Bach 7D or 7E and the Schilke 11A are popular mouthpieces with players who use the piccolo trumpet. Some piccolo trumpet mouthpiece receivers take a cornet shank and others use a trumpet shank. There may be difficulty with a few of the European instruments because some of these have a taper on the mouthpiece receiver which is different from the standard Morse No. 1 used by American manufacturers. A European trumpet may have to have a mouthpiece made with a custom shank if the standard unit which is supplied with the instrument is not satisfactory.

Choosing whether to play the instrument in A or B flat depends upon the key of the music being performed. A general rule for the decision is based on the concert pitch of the selection being played. If the piece is in a concert key with sharps in the signature, the piccolo is played in A. If the concert pitch is in a key with flats in the signature, the instrument is played in B flat. The decision when the signature has no sharps or flats would be based on the number of accidentals involved, special technical considerations (*i.e.* trills), and the ease of fingering patterns.

The piccolo trumpet may come with two lead pipes, one for A and the other for B flat. Others have only the B flat which extends for tuning in A. In either case, it is usually necessary to extend the valve slides slightly when playing the instrument in A so that the proper tuning is achieved.

Many piccolo trumpets have a fourth valve which lowers the pitch and extends the low register a perfect fourth. It serves as an alternate fingering for the valve combination 1-3. Since the combination 1-3 and 1-2-3 below the staff are quite sharp, the fourth valve may be used for 1-3 and 2-4 for 1-2-3.

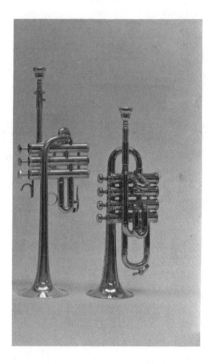

Fig. 53 Piccolo A-B flat Trumpets (three-valve, left; four-valve, righ)

The player who is unfamiliar with the blowing properties of the piccolo trumpet must be very sensitive to adjust the breath supply so as not to overblow the capacity of the instrument. It is important to remember that the bore size (.401–.410 inch) of most piccolo trumpets is appreciably smaller than the bores of *mezzo-soprano* trumpets (.450–.464 inch). Overblowing will produce an unpleasant, harsh tone.

Taking breaths which are too large also will fatigue the performer more rapidly than usual. At the end of a phrase there still will be some air left in the lungs. Most of the oxygen will have been absorbed out of this air and what remains is mostly carbon dioxide. If another breath is taken without expelling this residue, the player will have the feeling of suffocation from having too much, rather than too little breath.

An excellent book for introduction to this instrument is *The Piccolo Trumpet,* by David Hickman. This book contains preliminary exercises for adaptation to the trumpet, etudes, excerpts, and duets. Selmer also publishes an informative pamphlet, *The Piccolo B flat-A Trumpet* by Vincent Cichowicz of the Chicago Symphony Orchestra.

Explanation of the transpositions necessary with the piccolo trumpet are discussed in detail in the section on transposition. The following illustrations are excerpts from the orchestral repetoire which I feel are particularly adaptable to the piccolo trumpet.

Bach, J. S. *B Minor Mass*—(piccolo A)
Bach, J. S. *Brandenburg Concerto No. 2*—(piccolo B flat)
Bach, J. S. *Christmas Oratorio*—(piccolo A)
Bach, J. S. *Magnificat*—(piccolo A)
Bach, J. S. *Suite No. 3* and *No. 4*—(piccolo A)
Handel, G. F. *Judas Maccabaeus*—(piccolo A)
Handel, G. F. *Messiah*—(piccolo A)
Handel, G. F. *Royal Fireworks Music*—(piccolo A)
Handel, G. F. *Samson*—(piccolo A)
Handel, G. F. *Water Music*—(piccolo A)
Mussorgsky-Ravel "Samuel Goldenberg and Schmuyle" from *Pictures at an Exhibition*—(piccolo A)
Stravinsky, I. *Le Sacre du Printemps*—(piccolo B flat)
Stravinsky, I. *Petrouchka*—final muted duet (piccolo B flat)
Ravel, M. *Bolero*—ending (piccolo B flat)

The Piccolo C Trumpet

The four-valve piccolo C trumpet is the most recent addition to manufacturers' contributions to *sopranino* trumpets. The models all come with four valves as the piccolo C instrument by itself would be somewhat impractical because of the absence of low register. The fourth valve is in G and the slide may be pulled on some instruments to bring that down to G flat. Wilfreds Cardosa in his book, *High Trumpets, Vol. I–II,* claims, "This instrument practically makes all piccolos in all keys obsolete . . ." Perhaps this remains to be seen, as the development of the piccolo C is relatively new. However, it does seem that with the number of high trumpet works by J. S. Bach in F major, D major, and C major, this trumpet would gain widespread appeal.

Fig. 54 Piccolo C Trumpet

General Comments on Using the Fourth Valve on Higher Key Trumpets

There is some discrepancy as to what are the manufacturers' intentions and what happens in practical application of the fourth valve on some of the higher key trumpets. The chart on pg. 55 indicates the most common fingerings assuming the fourth valve actually lowers the fundamental a perfect fourth *and* extends the low register by the same amount when all four valves are lowered.

This sequence of pitches and fingerings is correct with *some* high trumpets. However, it should be noted that certain higher key trumpets with four valves suffer the same problems as some four valve flugelhorns. (See Chapter 11, "The Flugelhorn.") Since the length of the fourth valve slide is built in proportion to the other three valve slides, it may lower the open series a perfect fourth when the fourth valve is used by itself, but the pitches become progressively more sharp as descending chromatic fingering combinations are added. When the player reaches the combination 1-2-3-4, he finds he has not reached the expected perfect fourth below the combination 1-2-3, but in reality the interval has shrunk to a major third.

These tuning problems can often be corrected by extending the third or fourth valve slide, or by lowering the note with embouchure adjustment. The player who is aware of these shortcomings and will work conscientiously with a Stroboconn, will find that he is in a much better position to cope with the necessary corrections.

Conclusion

Trumpet players in symphony orchestras 40 years ago were concerned only with executing their parts on *mezzo-soprano* B flat trumpets. The respected players of that era must have been quite unique to be successful with modest equipment. At the same time, we cannot assume that trumpeters of today need to have less ability because there is a much wider instrument selection. Today orchestra seasons are longer, the schedules are more demanding, and composers are constantly writing at what often seems to be the technical limitations of the instrument. Orchestral trumpet players should consider themselves fortunate to have a wide selection of high trumpets to make their profession more feasible.

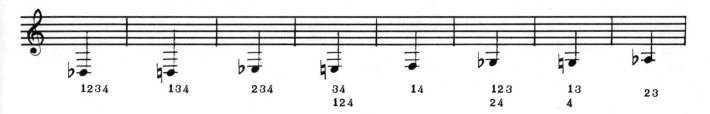

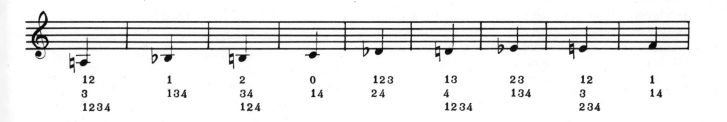

Chapter 14
Scales and Arpeggios

Scales and arpeggios are implemented into a student's early musical training and remain a part of that study, regardless of how many years he plays his instrument. Young students may see these only as busy work or obstacles they must pass before moving on to something interesting, but the professional player recognizes them as a necessity to unify all the techniques of a good performer. Scales and arpeggios usually represent only a small portion of the young student's practice time. The irony of the situation is the fact that most professional performers think the reverse; if practice time is limited, they will always see that scales and arpeggios have high priority on that time.

Practicing scales and arpeggios gives attention to many facets of musical performance at the same time: range, tone, articulation, breathing, dynamics, intonation, endurance, and musical style. These are discussed individually at the end of this section. My point at this time is that if students can be convinced of the benefits of scales, their musical training stands to progress faster.

I recommend that scales and arpeggios be incorporated into a practice routine immediately after the warm-up. In this way they assist in bringing together all the aspects of performing in good working order. They should represent approximately 15–20 percent of an individual's daily practice time. The student who does more than one practice session per day might wish to use scales and arpeggios after the warm-up in the first session and at the beginning of following sessions. This procedure should help the lip muscles become relaxed and agile in the later sessions.

Memorization

Memorization of scales and arpeggios should begin as soon as students begin to have control over the basic playing techniques of the trumpet. They should learn the key signatures and know how scales are constructed within those signatures. When memorizing, the scales and arpeggios should not be allowed to become mechanical, or worse yet, played in a hit-or-miss fashion. Students must always be thinking about where they are within the key, even though in time the act of repetition will turn some of the activity over to the subconscious (kinesthetic sensations).

Diatonic Scale Patterns

When a student has learned the major scales and can play all keys securely, he should advance to the major keys in a diatonic pattern. The diatonic pattern consists of playing the scale up one octave on each successive scale step.

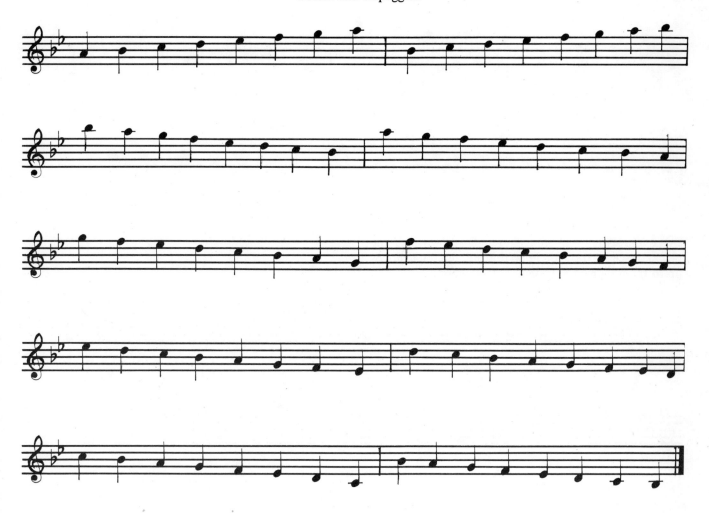

There may be range problems in some keys where the embouchure has not developed enough to cover the entire two octave span, but when this is the case, the scale is played sequentially through the fifth step, and the sixth and seventh steps approach the original tonic from below.

When playing this broken diatonic downward, the player descends through the sixth scale step, then moves up to the dominant and finishes from above.

Diatonic scales should also be played in the natural, harmonic, and melodic minors. Adapting the minor scales to the diatonic pattern should be quite easy after mastering the majors. Begin with the natural minor, which should present no problems as it is nothing more than starting on the sixth scale step of the previously learned majors. The harmonic form is the most difficult of the minors to play in the diatonic pattern. Mistakes are likely to happen at the augmented second which

comes between the sixth and seventh scale steps. Having students name the pitches before they attempt to play the scale serves as a helpful reminder, which I strongly advocate.

Diatonic scales may be practiced in major and minor using a variety of rhythmic patterns. Good examples of these are found in the scale section of Arban's *Complete Method*.

simile

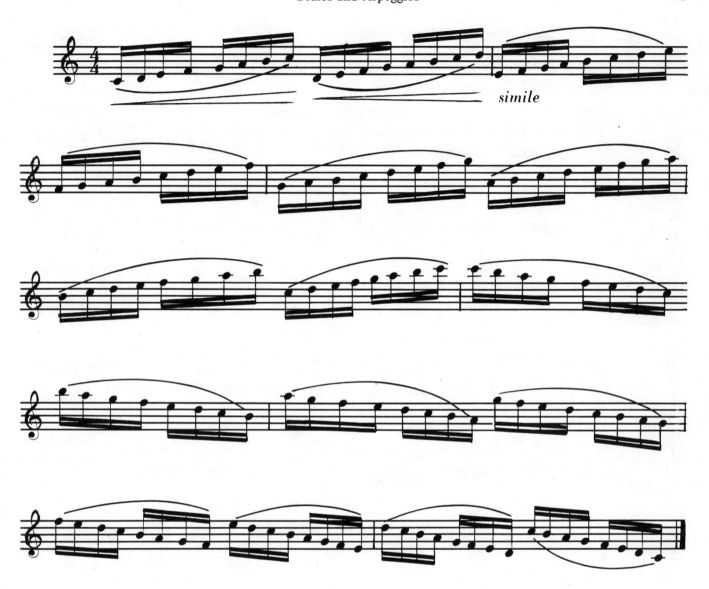

simile

Simple and Compound Rhythmic Patterns

Further variations of major and minor scales may be created by adding rhythmic patterns. To execute these patterns using one octave scales, an additional note must be added to both the top and the bottom of the scale so that it ends on the beat.

The scale may be now played in these common simple
meter variations:

The same scale format is adaptable to these familiar
compound rhythmic groupings:

Scales may be played with rhythmic variations over a two octave range by adding only the lower note to make the exercise end on the beat.

The pulse does not fall consistently on the tonic in the middle of these scales as it does in the one octave scales. The student should notice on what scale steps the beat comes in the second octave.

Quintuplet Groupings

Major and minor scales will be mastered further by practicing in quintuplet groupings. The one octave scale in quintuplets is played by adding two notes at the top and one at the bottom.

The same grouping over two octaves needs only the lower note added.

Diminished Scales

Performers interested in jazz and improvisation should also practice diminished scales. These are derived from the diminished seventh arpeggio. In one form they use a note a half step above all the arpeggio tones and in the other form they use a note a half step below all arpeggio tones. As there are only three diminished seventh chords if enharmonic spellings are used, there are only six different sets of pitches to be learned.

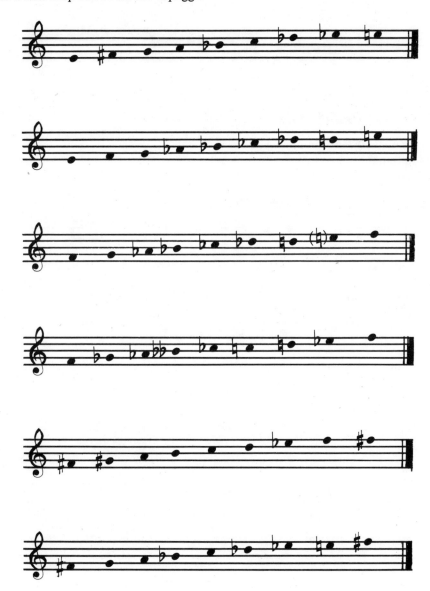

Whole Tone Scales

With enharmonic spellings, a player can know all the whole tone scales.

Scales in Thirds and Pedal Points

Additional facility will be gained by practicing the major and minor scales in thirds.

The same is true with lower and upper pedal points.

Arpeggios

Arpeggio practice can be introduced by having the student learn one octave and two octave (where possible) major, minor, major-minor sevenths, and diminished sevenths.

Straight: Major—One Octave

Minor—Two Octaves

Major-Minor Seventh—One Octave

Diminished Seventh—Two Octaves

The same arpeggios then are learned in broken patterns. They may be broken by triads.

Or broken by chord:

The arpeggios also may be broken in diatonic patterns:

Tone Quality

Work toward uniformity of tone quality throughout the scale range. Look for the center of the tone on each note so resonance is uniform. Practice with the lights turned off or your eyes closed. This can add a new dimension to your awareness of tone production.

Intonation

Scales and arpeggios should be practiced both with and without a *Stroboconn.* You should be especially aware of notes which need adjustments with the valve slides. Many times it is possible to lip these notes in tune, but the tone center is lost in the process.

Articulation

Take special care to produce identical articulations on each note. This necessitates using a variety of tongue positions, depending upon the register in which you are playing.

High Register

Avoid the tendency to let the teeth close as you ascend into the upper register. There also may be the problem of letting the bottom lip roll in. Keep the chin flat and firm the corners of the embouchure while ascending.

Low Register

Listen for consistent resonance, particularly in the range below the staff. Many times these notes are slighted because the jaw does not drop for additional resonance in the oral cavity. Be careful that the mouthpiece placement remains constant and is not allowed to shift into a different position when the aperture is opened further.

Endurance

Rest a moderate amount between scales, but only enough to keep the playing consistent. While working for endurance concentrate on relaxation and let the air and embouchure muscles produce a full tone.

Breath Control and Dynamics

Vary the space between breathing points in the scales and arpeggios. Practice using catch breaths (see Chapter 3, "Breathing") and work to improve their efficiency. Play at all the various dynamic ranges to pace the breath in relation to the dynamic.

Legato Control

Work to make the scales and arpeggios as smooth as possible. Play them slurred, legato tongued and a combination of both. Think of them as legato phrases—not merely drill exercises.

Conclusion

Scales and arpeggios cannot be expected to work miracles with an individual's performance, but conscientiously applied, they can make a significant difference in rate of improvement. Memorizing the scales allows the student to direct his total attention to playing fundamentals without the distraction of reading from the printed page.

Chapter 15

Vibrato

Tasteful use of vibrato on the trumpet and cornet can be a useful asset to enhance the tone quality. It is very important, however, to recognize when and to what degree it is musically acceptable to use the vibrato on these instruments.

String performers take it for granted that vibrato on their instruments is an inherent part of the tone—so much so that the hand begins the vibrato production before the bow is drawn on the string. The same is not true with the trumpet. Vibrato is used a relatively small percentage of the time. Players use it in legato, *cantabile* solo passages, in concert or stage band or in a solo performance. It is important to understand that the vibrato is not used in unison passages with more than one instrument or on a sustained chord. Vibrato in these instances will make it impossible to achieve correct intonation.

The concept of vibrato use and speed varies from country to country, but an acceptable speed in this country is five to seven times per second.

Although it is important to remember that a good vibrato can enhance a tone, this should not be taken to mean it can make a poor tone acceptable. It is necessary that correct habits in tone production be observed with or without vibrato.

Hand Vibrato

The hand vibrato is the most easily controlled type of vibrato on the trumpet. This is because the player has a visual, physical, and audible image of what is being produced. Either the hand is moving and the vibrato is being produced, or it is not.

With the hand vibrato, the performer must maintain complete relaxation of the right hand, wrist and forearm. The fingers on the valve caps and the thumb in position below the leadpipe where the first and second valves come together represent the contact with the instrument. The right elbow represents the contact point on the other end. Everything between these two points remains as relaxed as possible.

It is not uncommon for a student to have trouble relaxing the wrist. In this case it is advisable to have him move the wrist vertically. This is the more natural direction for the joint to move. After a few weeks of practice in this manner, the wrist should be free enough to move horizontally.

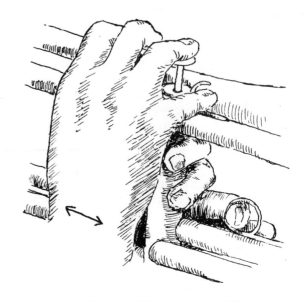

Fig. 55 Right Hand Motion for Hand Vibrato

One of the main assets of the hand vibrato is the variety of emphases that may be produced in this manner. It can range from a barely audible trace of color to a heavy, dominant influence on the tone. One might find it necessary to use the latter in stage band performance.

Lip Vibrato

The lip vibrato actually is produced by a synchronized motion of the lip and jaw. The jaw stays in its forward position (as discussed earlier in Chapter 4, Embouchure), but moves almost imperceptibly up and down. As the lip and jaw move, the performer will produce a change in both pitch and tone color.

In my opinion, the lip vibrato becomes a more integral part of the tone than any other type and for this reason I prefer that method. The hand vibrato, if not carefully controlled, can sound like an ornament which is superficially added to the tone. Many players, however, feel that the adjustment of the lip aperture, particularly in the upper register, gives them a feeling of insecurity.

Diaphragm Vibrato

The diaphragm vibrato is produced by creating a pulsating effect with the air column. You can feel this

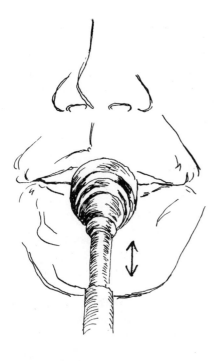

Fig. 56 Jaw Motion for Lip Vibrato

sensation by putting your hand in front of your mouth and breathing out using the syllables *H_aa, A_aa, A_aa.* (Giving emphasis when noted). The diaphragm vibrato is the least frequently used of the three methods. I have encountered some recognized brass teachers who advocate this form; however, they are usually trombone or tuba specialists. I tend to think the diaphragm vibrato may be somewhat more successful on those instruments because they have significantly less resistance than the trumpet.

Vibrato in Various Registers

It is important to understand that the emphasis of the vibrato being produced will vary significantly with the register of the passage being played. A student may be producing a well-controlled vibrato on a third space C on the staff. The same amount of vibrato used on the C below the staff will produce an effect which is much heavier. In a similar manner, an identical vibrato on the C above the staff will be barely audible. This factor must be taken into consideration when the performer is analyzing the overall impression he is trying to make.

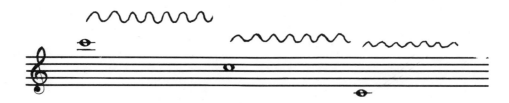

Teaching the Vibrato

A band director need not expect every trumpet student in the section to be able to produce a refined vibrato. Only those who will be doing solo performing or playing solo passages in ensembles will find it necessary. These students can begin to develop the technique in junior high school after the director is convinced they can play consistently with a controlled, sustained tone.

The technique for teaching the vibrato is similar, regardless of whether the student is learning the hand, lip, or diaphragm vibrato. Using the method discussed earlier for the particular type vibrato chosen, the student should begin with a straight tone, progressively add vibrato, and then gradually extract it from the sound.

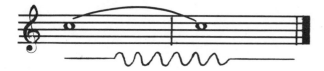

This can be practiced in steps on a scale in a moderate register. The student should strive to make the maximum amount of vibrato uniform on each note.

The next step is to begin and end the note with vibrato, but play with a straight tone in the middle.

There is one particular consideration which is unique to the beginning stages of the hand vibrato. When choosing a scale the student should be careful to pick a key which uses as few notes as possible that are fingered open. It is helpful to have some valves down to establish secure contact between the hand movement and the instrument. Students commonly will be somewhat distressed when first learning the hand vibrato because they feel insecure and uncomfortable with the pressure and release of the mouthpiece on the embouchure as the hand moves. Given a little practice, they will become oblivious to this.

Materials for Vibrato Practice

After students have learned to produce a vibrato which is controlled to the extent that they are completely aware as to whether or not they are using it, they will want some etudes for practical application. Anything of a non-technical, legato style is appropriate. I personally prefer "The Art of Phrasing" section from J. B. Arban's *Complete Method* (C. Fischer) or Concone's *Lyrical Studies* edited by Sawyer (The Brass Press).

Vibrato Errors

The most commonly found incorrect use of vibrato is the student who uses it continually and cannot play a note of even minimal duration without it. If we perceive the vibrato as an ornament to the tone an analogy might be to imagine a person who wears a large quantity of ·decorative jewelry at one time. It then becomes a detriment to the overall image, or at least loses its effect.

The student invariably is unaware that he has this habit. As a remedial measure it is helpful to use a tape recorder and have the student listen to his own playing. When it becomes obvious to him, he can then work on sustained long tones using an absolutely straight tone. Careful practice with this should correct the difficulty.

It is important to note that students who have this fault almost invariably use the lip vibrato.

Conclusion

Like so many aspects of successful musical performance, students must have a concept of the presence of a tasteful vibrato as part of the trumpet tone. These concepts can be established by teacher demonstration or by listening to live performers and recordings of respected players. Often students will find that it is necessary to actually listen intently for the vibrato. It is a good sign when this is the case. Obviously the performer has refined the vibrato to a point where the listener is only aware that the tone has a beautiful quality. This is the goal of a musically acceptable vibrato.

Chapter 16
Transposition

Trumpet students are fortunate to have a diverse selection of good quality literature for study and performance. While we may at times regret that many of the great composers did not write for our instrument, (a problem which pianists and string players do not face), we must consider ourselves fortunate to have material available which makes study of the trumpet challenging and interesting.

One area of study, however, must be considered mundane. That is mastery of transposition technique. One thing which should be reassuring to the student is that transposition is just as boring for the instructor as it is to the pupil. Having seen both sides of the case, I cannot say with surety who is in a position to find transposition study more tedious, the teacher or the student.

Perhaps this is the reason college instructors find that relatively few aspiring trumpeters entering undergraduate programs have any significant background in transposition. What is totally unforgivable is the student who applies to graduate school or seeks to secure a professional position with little or no background.

Transposition in Applied Music

The reasons for applied music students to work with transposition are obvious. The literature which they will be performing will, for the most part, need to be transposed. One must have a secure grasp of the technique—secure enough that it does not stand in the way of competent musical performance.

Some applied trumpet majors might try to use the rationale that in these days of a tight orchestral performance market, they are only interested in doing studio teaching or pursuing a graduate degree to enter the college teaching field. Therefore they assume studying transposition will only take time away from other areas which seem more important to them. This philosophy can only perpetuate an undesirable situation.

Transposition in Music Education

Transposition is equally important for music education majors. It will be used in score reading every day of their professional lives. Competency will give the conductor control of his work. A conductor must have mastery of the musical score in order to know quickly

and accurately exactly what pitches each instrument is playing.

Secondly, the music educator often will be called upon to demonstrate a musical phrase or articulation. Even though professionals have studied all the instruments at one time or another in pedagogy classes, it is much easier if they are able to illustrate by using their major instrument, as this will give the student the best example of their musical ideas.

Thirdly, most applied music teachers hope that after graduation, students will continue to perform on their instruments even if only to a small degree. The opportunities for orchestral performance in community and semi-professional orchestras are greater than ever. Any young music student is bound to hold his teacher in higher esteem if that teacher can be seen and heard as an active performer. The ability to transpose is essential for all levels of orchestral performance.

Another reason for studying transposition is proposed by Dr. Gordon Mathie, trumpet professor at the Crane School of Music, State University of New York at Potsdam. Dr. Mathie contends that transposition study tends to improve sight reading in musicians. Although he admits that judgment of this conclusion is subjective, I agree with his conclusion. As he mentions, the experienced music reader must transfer the printed notes seen on the page into sounds. While he is reading these, he is also hearing (or auralizing) in his mind before the audible production of these notes.

This is all part of the process of reading ahead and committing a portion of a passage to musical memory, if only for a moment. Work in transposition sharpens this element of musical perception.

Learning to transpose on the trumpet, or any instrument for that matter, is a technique which is learned and mastered by practice and application.

When mastered, one does not forget how to apply it, but unless transposition is used with regularity it may deteriorate. This is not unlike the total picture of playing the instrument.

Transposition by Interval

A melodic line may be transposed by interval, clef, or a combination of the two systems. When transposing by interval, the player simply raises or lowers the written notes by an appropriate interval (*i.e.,* up a major second

for a C trumpet part played on a B flat instrument,
up a perfect fourth for an E flat part on a B flat
instrument, etc.) It is also necessary to raise or lower
the key signature by the same interval.

Assume the following passage is to be played on a
B flat trumpet:

for C transposition the key would be changed:

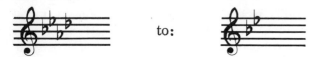

and the passage would be read:

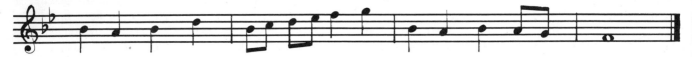

for D transposition the key would be changed:

and the passage would be read:

for E flat transposition the key would be changed:

and the passage would be read:

for E transposition the key would be changed:

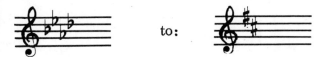   to:

and the passage would be read:

for F transposition the key would be changed:

   to:

and the passage would be read:

An exception in the interval system occurs when playing a part written for A trumpet on a B flat trumpet or any situation which requires transposing down a half-step. In any flat key the conventional interval system is used. In the key of no sharps or flats, or any sharp key, the part may be lowered by changing the key signature and reading the notes as the written pitches. (*i.e.* C becomes C flat; B becomes B flat; etc.) It is still necessary to alter accidentals, however, so sharps become naturals, naturals become flats, and flats become double flats.

Trumpet in A

as played on a B flat trumpet:

Trumpet in A

as played on a B flat trumpet:

Transposition by Clef

Transposition by clef is probably the least commonly used system by trumpet performers. Some teachers believe the reason for this is that trumpet students begin reading in the treble clef and it is usually quite some time before they become exposed to piano or *solfeggio*. Some European trumpet players begin *solfeggio* studies concurrently with initial instruction on their instrument. Learning transposition seems to be less difficult for them. Those who transpose by clef use a clef for each transposition (*i.e.* alto clef to play a C trumpet part on a B flat trumpet).

A more common alternative to using either the interval system or the clef system exclusively is to use a combination of the two. Opinions vary among teachers as to which system is easiest for each transposition.

The chart on pg. 79 shows each of the common transpositions as it relates to the B flat trumpet. The B flat instrument is illustrated since that is the most common trumpet for a student to be playing when he begins the study of transposition. Each key shows the clef relationship to accomplish the appropriate transposition.

Clef Transpositions as Used on a B flat Trumpet

In addition to the clef or interval techniques, I feel that students should be encouraged to look at the music analytically for anything which might allow them to have more facility in reading. Some of these things could include diatonic patterns, straight and broken arpeggiated figures, and melodic sequences.

Beginning Teaching Steps

Dr. Mathie and Dr. Norbert Carnovale both suggest preparing a student for transposition study by playing scales in thirds, fourths, and other interval patterns and arpeggiated figures in all keys. They should also play familiar tunes in several different keys.

A logical following step is to transpose simple songs which have a strong tonal feeling, but are not familiar to the student. This will necessitate actually transposing and not merely relying on the ear to recognize pitches. At the same time their tonal nature will make missed notes readily apparent. A good source for these songs is "The Art of Phrasing" section of the *Complete Method* by Arban/Goldman. Some of the duets in the same book provide interesting challenges for students who want to practice sightreading transposition together.

Following the beginning efforts, students may use either *The Orchestra Trumpeter*, by Sigmund Hering or *100 Etudes for Transposition* by Ernest Sachse. My procedure is to begin with C transposition for a few weeks, subsequently adding A transposition. After gaining security in these two keys, the first studies should be played in more difficult transpositions, for instance D, E flat and A flat, while continuing on the more advanced studies in A and C. The remaining transpositions of E, G alto and F alto are then added to the first studies as a final step. With this sequence, the student may be working simultaneously from three or more sections of the book.

Cafarelli's *One Hundred Melodic Studies* and Bordogni's *Twenty-Four Vocalises* are both challenging in that the transposing keys change occasionally or con-

Clef Tranpositions as Used on a B flat Trumpet

Trumpet in A
Tenor Clef

Trumpet in A flat
Tenor Clef

Trumpet in B flat
Treble Clef

Trumpet in C
Alto Clef

Trumpet in D
Bass Clef

Trumpet in E flat
Mezzo-Soprano Clef

Trumpet in E
Mezzo-Soprano Clef

Trumpet in F
Baritone Clef

stantly throughout the etude. This provides a continual challenge to stay alert and not rely on playing by ear.

I do not wait until a student has completed the study of transposition before adding orchestral excerpts. After the less complicated keys are mastered, some well-chosen excerpts may be introduced. This provides the student with a clearer idea of the practical application and serves as incentive for work on the more difficult keys.

Piccolo A-B flat Trumpet Transpositions

More frequent use of the piccolo A-B flat trumpet has created some transposition demands that were not encountered a few years ago. (Choice of the A or B flat trumpet is discussed in the Chapter 13, "The Higher-Key Trumpets.") It would be impossible to illustrate all the transposition examples which might be appropriate for that instrument. The illustrations below show the common transpositions necessary when using the piccolo A-B flat.

Written for trumpet in D

as played on the A piccolo trumpet:

Written for trumpet in F

as played on the B flat piccolo trumpet:

Written for trumpet in C

as played on the A piccolo trumpet:

The chart below shows ways of indicating the common transpositions:

English	French	Italian	German
In G	en Sol	in Sol	in G
in A♭	en La♭	in La♭	in As
	en La bémol	in La bemolle	
in A	en La	in La	in A
in B♭	en Si♭	in Si♭	in B
	en Si bémol	in Si bemolle	
in B	en Si	in Si	in H
in C	in Ut	in Do	in C
in D	en Re	in Re	in D
in E♭	en Mi♭	in Mi♭	in Es
	en Mi bémol	in Mi bemolle	
in E	en Mi	in Mi	in E
in F	en Fa	in Fa	in F

Chapter 17
Multiple Tonguing

The technique of double and triple tonguing should be mastered by all serious students of the cornet and trumpet. This is true even though multiple tonguing is used much less extensively than when cornet solos were in vogue. During that era it was a forgone conclusion that every piece of virtuoso solo literature had a variation utilizing double or triple tonguing—sometimes a variation for each. The fact that performers today are called upon less frequently to use multiple tonguing has caused some instructors to eliminate teaching it altogether.

Neglecting multiple tonguing should not be the case. Occasions when it is needed demand it be executed with the utmost in precision and clarity.

Needless to say, it is important for the student to have control of a rapid, clear single tongue before multiple tonguing is introduced. The ultimate goal of multiple tonguing is to duplicate a series of rapid single articulations. However, with multiple tonguing, the potential for speed is greater and less effort is expended.

It makes no difference whether double or triple tonguing is introduced first. In fact, some teachers will introduce and teach both simultaneously. More often the choice is decided by the solo or ensemble demands on a student at a given time.

The articulation syllables for double tonguing are *tŭ-kŭ*. (The *ŭ* sound is as in the word up.)

The common syllables for triple tonguing are *tŭ-tŭ-kŭ*.

The main difficulty with either double or triple tonguing is the uncomfortable feeling when producing the *kŭ* syllable with the back (pharyngeal) section of the tongue. (For more detail on the sections of the tongue, see Chapter 6, "Articulation.") Invariably the *kŭ* syllable always comes out weaker and less clear than the *tŭ* syllable. The student has been using the front of

the tongue since he was introduced to the instrument and it is understandable that the *kŭ* syllable produced by the pharyngeal section will be completely new and undeveloped.

Some teachers believe that a better balance in the relative strengths of the articulation is achieved by placing the *kŭ* in the middle of the triplet.

Regardless of whether the *kŭ* syllable comes at the end of the group as the third articulation or in the middle of the group, the teacher and student must realize the object is not to hide the *kŭ* articulation. The *kŭ* must be sharpened and strengthened to the point of being indistinguishable from the *tŭ*.

There are some teachers who favor using the double tonguing syllables for triple tonguing as in this example:

These same teachers contend that it is then necessary to learn only one technique—double tonguing. While this idea has merit, my own experience with it has been that long continuous lines of the articulation become more difficult to hold steady. I should also add that I have never found a student who felt comfortable enough using it that they did not feel it was necessary to learn the more common *tŭ-tŭ-kŭ* system as well. Thus any argument for time saving is negated.

As mentioned before, my theory on production of the *k* syllable is that it is produced by the back section of the tongue. Students will often have a tendency to produce the *k* syllable in the throat. This incorrect approach will lead to a distorted tone and will limit the tempo at which the multiple tonguing can be executed.

The student should not only work to develop the multiple tonguing at various speeds, but with various strengths. The dynamic strength must vary from a light articulation, like that used in some cornet solos, to a heavy forceful tongue, as with some symphonic literature.

Teaching Multiple Tonguing

The first step in teaching multiple tonguing is done without the instrument. The student holds his hand a few inches in front of his mouth and used the tongue to produce the syllable *tă* or *tŭ*. A small impulse of air will be felt against the palm of the hand.

Fig. 57 Feeling the Air Impulse on the Hand

Next, the same exercise should be done using the syllable *kă* or *kŭ*. Try to get the same velocity to the air impulse on both the *t* and *k* syllables. If the back of the tongue drops quickly, the effect will be achieved successfully.

When it is possible to produce both syllables with identical strength, play the following exercise with the normal single articulation.

etc.

The same exercise is then played with the *t-k* syllables at the same tempo. Next the exercise is played using only the *k* syllable on all the notes. Lastly, back to the single tonguing articulation to re-establish the ideal for comparison.

It is very important to remember the sustained note at the beginning and end of the exercise. A common fault for many people is that multiple tonguing becomes too choppy.

Using the sustained note helps to convey the concept of the continuity of the air stream. This continuity is maintained throughout the multiple articulation with no feeling of detachment. Separating the notes at this stage of development will only restrict the maximum tempo and smoothness later.

It should be noted that the reiteration of these single pitches should be restricted to notes in a comfortable register. Trying to play this exercise too high or low in the beginning will only cause frustration.

After both syllables are being produced clearly and evenly, the tempo gradually may be increased. One

pitfall for which both the teacher and student should be alert as the tempo increases is the false emphasis which may begin to occur on the *t* syllable. If this stress becomes evident, there is no alternative but to go back and slow down the tempo until this emphasis is eliminated.

Material for multiple tonguing practice can be found in several method books including Arban and St. Jacome. Only reiterated pitches should be played during the first few weeks of study. Attempting exercises which move diatonically or in arpeggiated patterns too soon will only preoccupy the player with technical demands and distract attention from the basic goals of uniformity and clarity.

The various positions of the tongue were discussed in the section on articulation. The same principles apply to multiple tonguing: the $\bar{u}$ or $\overline{oo}$ syllable is used in the low register, $\breve{a}$ in the staff, and $\overline{ee}$ above the staff. A good example of the application of this principle occurs in the trumpet call from Rimsky-Korsakoff's *Capriccio Espagnol.*

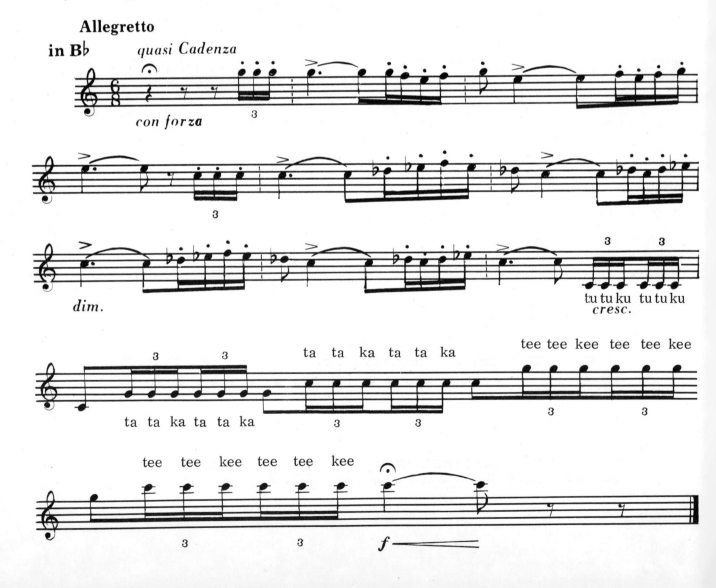

With this technique, the velocity of the air assists in producing the notes in the various registers.

Students have mastered the technique of miltiple tonguing if they can begin a long line of repeated notes with a single tongue, gradually accelerate smoothly and evenly into a double or triple tongue to maximum speed, and then decelerate to the original slow speed with the single tongue. This is similar to percussionists practicing the long roll and the goals are the same. When listening to the percussionist, one should not be aware as the player changes from the single stroke to the bounce. Likewise, the trumpet player should make his switch to and from the multiple articulation imperceptible.

Double tonguing exercise:

Triple tonguing exercise:

Complete control of multiple tonguing should include mastery of various strengths of articulation. A near legato *dă-gă* articulation might be used in the following example from Rimsky-Korsakoff's *Scheherazade.*

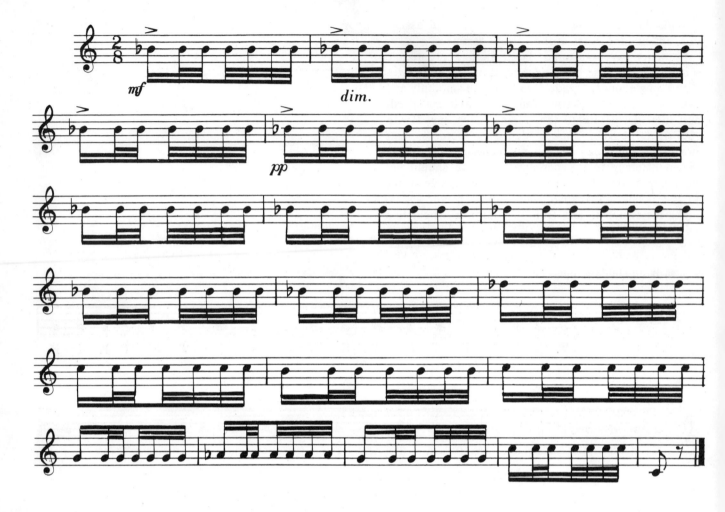

At the other end of the spectrum would be a heavy, *marcato* style at a loud dynamic which would be necessary in another section of the same composition.

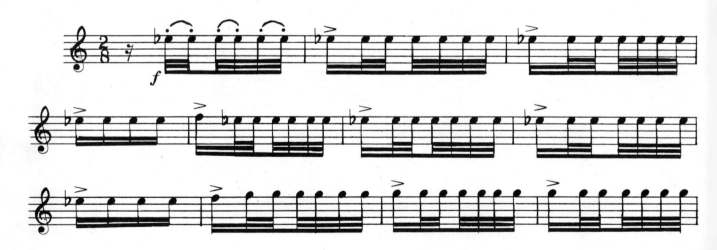

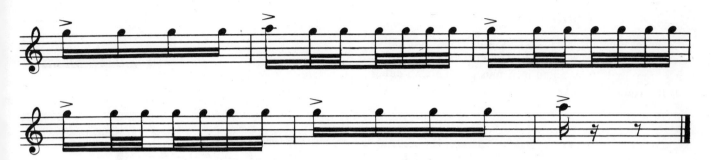

The performer who has complete control of multiple tonguing should be able to begin a series of notes with either a *t* or *k* syllable. If a passage which would normally be double tongued contains an uneven number of notes, it might well be most practical to start that passage with a *k* articulation. A practical application of this technique can be found in the following excerpt from Stravinsky's *Firebird*.

An individual might also choose to use multiple tonguing to solidify certain rhythmic figures. The dotted eighth note followed by a sixteenth note is always difficult to play with the correct rhythmic relationship between the two notes. This is particularly true if the tempo is fast. I have found that by double tonguing the notes, it is possible to keep the rhythmic relationship of these notes much more accurate.

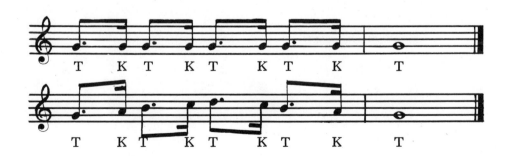

Flutter Tonguing

Flutter tonguing is a technique which is seldom called for, but the performer must be able to execute it when it is required. It is noted in a musical score in either of the following ways:

   or   

The technique for producing a flutter tongue is the same as the singer uses to roll the syllable *r*. The back of the tongue is fairly high and the tip of the tongue stays relaxed. As air passes over the tongue, the tip is allowed to flutter in the airstream. The secret to making the flutter tongue work is to keep the tip as relaxed as possible. If the tongue is relaxed and still will not produce the desired flutter, try using more air moving through the mouth. Consistent practice will help the student overcome any difficulties.

Chapter 18
Intonation Adjustments

It is impossible to overemphasize how important it is for an individual to be aware of the playing characteristics of his instrument. These include tone color, response, resistance, and certainly intonation deficiencies. Manufacturers have devoted countless amounts of time and money to research and improve the instrument, but there are still tuning problems which are present in the most highly-developed trumpets and cornets. Although these vary with the different instrument makes, there are some universal problem areas on all instruments. (Please be reminded that these comments refer only to the B flat trumpet. Intonation problems are different on trumpets in keys other than the *mezzo-soprano* B flat and are discussed in their appropriate chapters.)

Valve Slide Relationships

The greatest tuning problems on trumpets and cornets are due to the length of the various valve slides. The slides on the instrument are designed so they associate most closely with the open instrument sounding a concert B flat. Depressing the second valve adds enough tubing to lower the pitch by a half-step. There is no difficulty when the relationship is quite close to the open instrument; however, the problem becomes more difficult when the valve combinations become more complex, particularly the 1-3 and the 1-2-3 fingerings. While these slides individually may be nearly in tune with the open instrument, putting two or more together complicates the situation.

The problem may be understood more easily when compared to the trombone. As that instrument is played downward chromatically, the various slide positions become farther apart—thus the distance between the first and second positions is smaller than from the sixth to seventh positions.

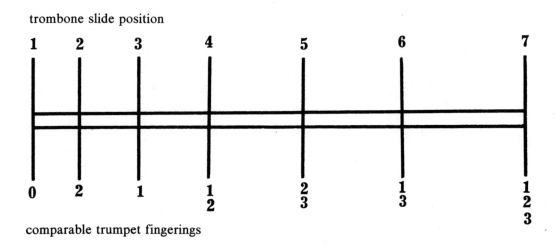

trombone slide position

comparable trumpet fingerings

The trombonist is free to place the slide wherever necessary to correct the intonation, but the trumpet player is more restricted by the valves.

Fifth Harmonic

Another common area for questionable intonation on the cornet and trumpet is the fifth harmonic (written fourth space E). This pitch is flat on most instruments. A detailed acoustical description of why this note is flat may be found in *The Inside Story of Brass Instruments,* by Dr. Earle E. Kent, published by C. G. Conn.

On most B flat trumpets and cornets the fifth harmonic can be satisfactorily *lipped-up* to the correct pitch. Using the possible alternate valve combination 1-2 gives a tone quality which is inconsistent with the remainder of the instrument. The sound is less clear and response is more difficult. The trumpeter must practice lipping-up this note and develop the ability to play it in tune.

The same intonation problem exists on the C trumpet, to an even greater degree. Here it is often necessary to use the 1-2 valve combination. As the pitch on this combination is somewhat sharp, the performer needs to compensate a small amount by using the trigger or thumb saddle on the first valve slide to lower it to the proper pitch level.

Other Modes of Vibration

Another note commonly having questionable intonation is the *A* above the staff. This *A* is somewhat sharp on most B flat trumpets and cornets. The note can be lowered easily by adjusting the first valve slide the amount necessary.

The high A is sharp to a greater degree on the C trumpet. The note may be lowered on this instrument as well by extending the first slide or if the pitch discrepancy is too great, the performer may finger the note with the third valve. This slide is long enough to make pitch low enough without further compensation. (For additional clarification see the B♭-C trumpet intonation chart in Chapter 12, "The C Trumpet.")

Although it is possible to make general statements concerning notes which commonly present intonation problems, I cannot overemphasize that these vary with different makes of instruments. It is up to the individual players, with assistance from their teacher and a *Stroboconn,* to determine how much each of these notes needs to be adjusted in order to play with consistently correct intonation.

A sensitive performer in an ensemble will also be alert to tuning adjustments that are necessary as changes in scoring, dynamics, instrumentation, temperature, and other factors occur during a concert. Alterations also may be necessary within a single selection. It is not unusual that an orchestral string section will tend to play somewhat sharp in the high positions on the fingerboard. Woodwinds can have notorious intonation difficulties in the upper register, and brasses will often play slightly flat in loud passages.

It is asking too much of any player to be constantly changing with each variable. However, a sensitive trumpet performer should be expected to adjust within reason as the situation demands.

Special intonation problems are encountered when muting the cornet and trumpet and are discussed in Chapter 25, "Mutes."

Chapter 19

How to Practice

It is important that every student and teacher take time to talk about an organized practice routine. All too often this discussion does not come about until the teacher detects something wrong in a student's progress, or the student reaches the frustration of an impasse and seeks advice.

It is just as important for the teacher to be aware that while general guidelines for practice may be laid down, each student's approach to the instrument differs, and a practice routine must be tailored to that individual's strengths and weaknesses. The discussion should include how to use practice time constructively, what to practice, and how long to practice.

Preparation for the Warm-Up

Before starting the warm-up, the student should have his instrument in proper playing condition. Included in this playing condition would be having the mouthpiece clean, the valves oiled and the instrument and mouthpiece up to playing temperature. (See Chapter 27, "Fundamental Repair," for more details on the first two points.) The instrument can be brought up to temperature by blowing warm air into the mouthpiece receiver for a few seconds. At the same time, hold the mouthpiece in the hand to bring it up to body temperature. These steps will assure the player that the tuning, tone, and response of the instrument will always be the same.

It is also important that the player be in the proper frame of mind before actually beginning the warm-up. All thoughts other than those immediately connected with satisfactory performance on the instrument must be set aside. The degree of success a player has through his practice day may well be determined by a satisfactory warm-up. Consequently it is important that all mental faculties be sharp and all concentration directed to the work to be done.

The Warm-Up

I feel that one word can be used to describe the initial phase of the warm-up—moderation. Moderation includes playing notes in a moderate range, at a moderate dynamic, and of a moderate length. Approaching the warm-up in this manner will avoid over-taxing the lip muscles during the critical first few minutes. The book which I prefer to use for warm-up exercises is Max Schlossberg's *Daily Drills and Technical Studies*. In the initial stages of playing, I normally limit my selection of exercises to those found on the first six pages of this book.

After some preliminary long-tone drills, repeated articulation studies are used to promote the free movement of the tongue. The articulations may be based on scale studies and should follow a sustained note.

The purpose of the sustained note is to establish the free flow of air needed to develop the maximum amount of resonance on the repeated notes.

While working on these elementary long-tone and articulation exercises, it is important to be aware of the sequence of breathing and articulation. After the breath is taken in it is immediately released into the instrument. There should be no hesitation between the inhalation and exhalation. (Detailed discussion of this is given in Chapter 3, "Breathing.") The next logical step in the warm-up is the implementation of simple lip slurs—again with moderation being the watch-word.

These are started in the staff and then expanded in three steps as indicated by the following exercise.

Note: Play each line using all seven chromatic valve combinations.

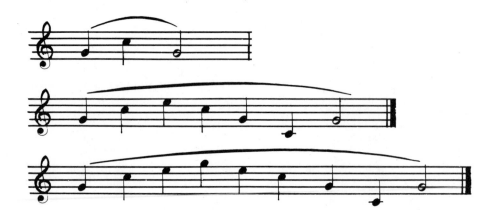

If the articulation response still seems sluggish at this point, the above exercise can be played with legato, marcato, and staccato tonguing before advancing to something more difficult.

I next use expanded scales to begin extending the range into the high and low registers. The expanded scales consist of patterns which include one note above the tonic on the top and one note below on the bottom. In the beginning stages of practice these are played in steady quarter note patterns.

When something more complex is desired, the same tonal compass may be incorporated into various simple and compound rhythmic patterns. (See Chapter 14, "Scales and Arpeggios," for a description of these rhythmic patterns on scales.)

The same concept may be used to further expand the range by going to a 10th above and a 4th below the starting note.

The basic purpose of this drill is to break the student's habit of thinking that an exercise always has to fit within an octave compass. After slurring and tonguing these exercises in several keys, the initial preparation phase of the warm-up is complete.

The previously outlined procedure should take about 20 minutes. It is quite possible to play all the material in less time; however, I believe that rest should be interspersed frequently in the warm-up. Some pedagogical books advocate alternating equal amounts of playing and resting throughout a practice session. This is a luxury few performers can afford. In addition to the time factor, this procedure has shortcomings in endurance development. However, I am convinced it is important to try to use this equal play and rest principle in the warm-up.

If it becomes necessary to warm-up in less than 20 minutes, the student should keep in mind that the play-rest distribution still should be observed. The time can be shortened by using fewer exercises, not a faster sequence. If the rest periods are shortened or eliminated during this critical time, the student undoubtedly will suffer from premature fatigue.

I recommend 20 minutes as a reasonable amount of time to spend on a warm-up. This should allow enough time for the embouchure, tongue, and breathing muscles to work efficiently. Naturally, some differences from this figure will be found among various students. The one hazard I strongly caution against is the idea some students have that it is necessary to have a prolonged warm-up, sometimes as much as two hours. Spending two hours with warm-ups does no good for the player. At the same time it takes time and energy away from developing other essential aspects of playing.

Post Warm-Up Routine

After these initial exercises, the player has the choice of continuing in one of two directions; beginning to work on lesson material—etudes, solos, transpositions, etc.—or working on drills to develop flexibility, technique, and finesse. I prefer the latter direction.

My personal choice for technical development at this point would be to select some of the drill material from Herbert L. Clark's *Technical Studies*. These may be slurred as written, single tongued, or multiple tongued. Extra challenge may be added by practicing them with a dotted eighth-sixteenth note rhythmic pattern or changing the key. (The second study works well in a minor key.) I caution students not to become frustrated if they cannot play the exercises with as many repetitions as the introductory notes indicate. One must keep in mind that they are being practiced with today's concept of performance, and this requires a fuller tone. These studies were originally intended to be played with a soft, subdued sound which required very little air. The tone had a light, almost whispered quality which was quite effective on cornet solo passages in the early 20th century. For these exercises to be applicable to today's playing, they should be practiced with a full, resonant tone and this uses the air supply much more quickly.

Additional technical exercises may be played from any of several sections of the Arban/Goldman *Complete Method*. Among these I would recommend the scale studies, chromatic studies, and broken scale patterns— all with various single and multiple articulations and with slurring combinations.

The next segment of practice should include some flexibility drill using either the Walter Smith *Lip Flexibility Studies,* or Charles Colin's *Lip Flexibility Studies.* (How to use these studies is discussed in Chapter 7, ''Legato Playing.'')

As a third and final step in the post warm-up, I recommend some of the later technical studies in the Schlossberg book, some arpeggio or interval studies, or some of the many drills in Robert Nagel's *Speed Studies*. Students wishing to cope with a real challenge may transpose some of the Nagel studies.

From 35 to 45 minutes is a practical amount of time to spend on the post warm-up routine. These exercises may be played in a more rapid sequence than the preliminary warm-up. If the player has elected to go immediately from the warm-up to lesson material, he should realize that the drill practice mentioned in this section should be done later in the daily routine. Practicing these advanced warm-ups is essential for building and maintaining technique, tone, accuracy, and endurance.

Etude Practice

Assuming a student is on a weekly lesson schedule, a few minutes should be taken at the beginning of the practice week to analyze the most effective sequence to prepare the assigned material.

Review Material

In most cases there will be old material re-assigned for further refinement, and new etudes. It is hoped that the teacher has made clear, constructive suggestions for improvements on the material to be repeated. The review of old material should be started early in the practice week before ideas begin to be forgotten. With these studies, individual sections should be practiced with difficult passages receiving special attention. The majority of one's review time should be spent on these particular sections, with perhaps the study only being played through completely once each day to maintain the feeling of continuity.

New Material

New material is approached in a different manner. It is important for the teacher to spend a few minutes at the end of a lesson to give the student an overview of the musical ideas and goals toward which he should be working. This overview should not be confused with trying to think for the student to the point where no ingenuity or creative thought is necessary on the student's part. The amount of time and detail on this aspect of the lesson varies with the level of advancement and capabilities of the student.

It is wise to begin only one new study of any length and difficulty in a given day. A person saturating himself with everything new at once will only encounter frustration. On the first playings, the student should try to determine the overall musical concepts of the study, phrase relationships, and sections which contain specific technical or musical problems. After this overview is established, the etude may be divided for detailed study. When improvement comes in these sections, the work can be practiced in its complete form again. Regardless of how much time in a practice period is spent on details, portions of the study should be practiced in their entirety each day. Practicing in unified sections serves as a reminder of the overall musical style.

All teachers of music have lamented the fact that "students don't know how to practice." The ability to dissect an etude and put it back together in better form is not something most students have instinctively. In many cases, we as teachers confuse inefficient work with what we might think is a student with only marginal talent.

Transposition

The technique of transposition is discussed extensively in Chapter 16, "Transposition," but I believe it is worth noting here that there is one unique aspect to efficient transposition practice. I recommend that students spend the first two or three days of their practice week working on transpositions without the instrument. This way they are not merely conditioning themselves to learn the exercises by rote. They must actually think the note by interval or clef relationship without assistance from their instrument. Practicing without the trumpet is also a constructive way to use a break in practice time while resting the embouchure.

Solos and Excerpts

As a systematic practice routine is developed, there will be times within this schedule that all the aspects of playing seem to work at their best. This time might be determined by the hour of the day, the mental attentiveness, the embouchure condition or other factors. I believe that solo and excerpt practice should be placed in the practice schedule during the period when the player is at a physical, mental, and psychological peak. Excerpts and solos are most closely related to performance demands and they should be studied when work can be the most constructive.

One of the prominent brass authors of today recommends that the excerpts be placed at the end of one's practice period. If the difficult passages can be played several times when the embouchure is fatigued, he believes that it becomes much easier to play them when the embouchure is fresh. This gives the performer the advantage of being able to work at his best even with the added anxiety of playing for an audience.

While I agree this theory has merit, it should also be noted that if a player consistently misses a note or passage (perhaps because of normal embouchure fatigue), in very little time he will begin to doubt his ability to play that particular passage. If allowed to continue, this doubt can destroy the confidence of even an experienced performer.

Endurance Exercises

Exercises for building endurance must be treated with caution. They are not unlike medicine which a doctor may prescribe. A teaspoon regularly will cure you—an overdose may cause you to become sicker.

The endurance building exercise I recommend is shown in the example below.

Practice sempre forte and with written dynamics

The exercise is from the quarter note scale studies near the beginning of the Arban book. Other Arban drills would also be acceptable. To avoid having detrimental side effects the following rules should be observed:

1. The drills should be limited to no more than three or four lines.
2. Frequent rest is imperative. At the end of each exercise you should rest *at least* as long as you have just played.
3. The drills are played with a full fortissimo tone, but at no time should the sound become uncontrolled.
4. The time allotted to these drills should be *no more* than five minutes total in any single practice session—playing and resting combined.

These exercises should build endurance if practiced over a few months. If the player finds that the stamina drops off appreciably, the tone loses its center, or the response becomes a problem, he should shorten or omit the drills for a few days.

The Warm-Down

At the close of a particularly strenuous practice session or rehearsal, it is helpful to include a few minutes for warming-down before putting the instrument away. The exercises are similar to the initial warm-up drills which began the day. Their purpose is to allow you to reconstruct the proper concepts of tone, breathing, and articulation.

If response is a problem at the close of a day of practice, it is helpful to play an exercise such as the following without using the tongue. The tone is started on each note using only the breath.

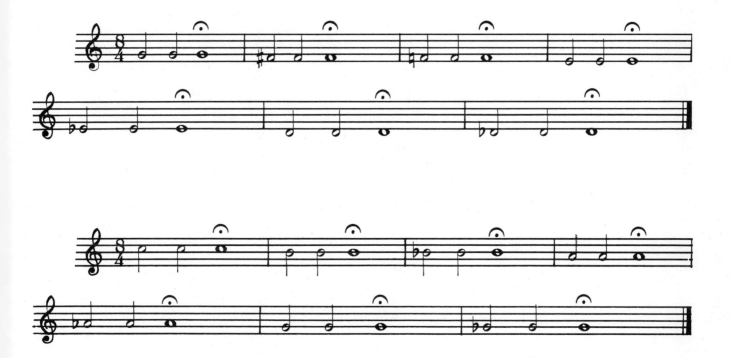

Normally, the accurate response of notes is derived by a coordinated effort from the breath and the tongue. Omitting the tongue provides an opportunity to examine how efficiently the breath is functioning. After a few minutes of this drill, the tongue is then returned to the normal articulation procedure and the problem is usually corrected.

Conclusion

Many professional musicians comment that they are able to accomplish constructive practice in considerably less time than they needed when they were students. It is essential that brass players learn to do this early in their careers. Pianists and string players are able to practice six, eight, or more hours a day. It is possible for them to devote large amounts of time because they are using the large muscles of the hands and arms. Brass players use lip muscles which have far less stamina and strength than the large muscles. Consequently they never develop the endurance to work constructively for these long periods of time. When a trumpet student learns to allot his time properly, his playing will progress much faster.

Chapter 20
Solo and Audition Preparation and Performance

There are some students who are content with the musical experiences derived from participating as a member of a large performing organization, but many will wish to play solo performances or audition for select ensembles.

This chapter is directed to those individuals. The theories discussed are applicable to the high school student going to a solo contest or to the college graduate seeking a professional orchestra position. Mental pressures and anxieties are similar at all levels of musical performance.

Preparation

One of the most detailed formats for performance preparation is delineated in Volume III of the Maier edition of the Arban method (Alfonse-Leduc). After considerable advance preparation there is a gradual reduction in practice time beginning three weeks before a solo performance. The day before the contest the individual warms-up and plays the solo through once. The contest day includes only a warm-up prior to appearance. While the system has considerable merit, I cannot completely endorse this format because I feel the performer's endurance will suffer if the tapering off is too prolonged.

The error which many students make is to reverse the process and not allow themselves enough preparation time. As the performance deadline nears, they continually increase the amount of time spent on the audition material. The intensified practice increases the feeling of anxiety and is certain to encourage apprehension.

Performance Material

The student and teacher should mutually reach a decision as to what repertoire is chosen. When the specific repertoire is selected, the teacher should judge whether the student is sufficiently advanced to play the material. If the choice is left to the student, he inevitably picks a selection which is too difficult for his level of achievement at that time. While there are some positive aspects to the selection of challenging repertoire, the student should not be allowed to attempt something for which he is not equipped.

An individual can exhibit the strong points of his technique and musicianship if a choice of material is allowed. If high range has not progressed to the same degree as tone production, naturally a solo which favors the latter should be selected.

After a mutually satisfactory choice has been made, a systematic plan is formulated for study of the material. The maximum amount of preparation and detailed study should be scheduled well in advance of the performance. If the material is mastered sooner than expected, there is the opportunity for some "trial runs." The solo may then be temporarily set aside so that it doesn't become stale and dull.

It is essential at the beginning of intensive study that the student have a clear overview of the concept and style of the material. Without this understanding, the goals of the student and teacher might be completely opposite to each other. The teacher should initially point out places of special concern or spots which might be beyond the student's understanding.

If the music has a piano accompaniment, it should be given to the pianist well in advance of the first rehearsal. Making the music available to them allows adequate preparation time prior to the first rehearsal with the soloist. It is very unnerving to have a solo prepared to performance tempo, only to regress to practice tempo while the accompanist learns the part. Not only does this waste time, but it can have a negative effect on the success of the finished presentation.

The soloist and accompanist must agree on the musical style early in their preparation. They then work on concepts as well as technique in their individual preparation from the beginning and they will create a much more satisfactory working relationship.

If recordings are available of the solo or audition material, these should be studied. Listening to a professional performance is worth more than several hours of practice. It is even better if there is more than one recording of the work as studying a variety of concepts will undoubtedly provide some contrasting musical ideas. The student should seek to find ideas from other performances which can complement his own, rather than try to merely duplicate the recorded performance. An exception to this might be the person preparing for a specific orchestral audition. Finding recordings by the conductor of the ensemble for which a player is auditioning will give insight into the conductor's interpretation of specific works and styles. This concept should be duplicated as closely as possible.

The acoustics of the room have an effect on the success of a performance. If possible, one should play in the performance room well in advance of the program. The performer then has an opportunity to get accustomed to the acoustics of the room and anticipate adjustments in dynamics and style that may have to be made.

A room which has considerable reverberation and is very *live* will sometimes make a performer feel as though he is playing too loudly. The first reaction is to decrease the dynamics. The scope of dynamic contrast is then reduced and response will be jeopardized because the individual is trying to play too softly.

If the room has an abundance of sound absorbing material the tone will seem very *dead*. The performer may find that he tires quickly from constantly trying to produce more sound. There is little that the player can do to compensate for the acoustics in a *dead* room; however, a general recommendation would be to face the audience more directly and concentrate on centering the tone as much as possible.

If it is impossible to play in the room before the performance, at least walk out on the stage and observe the surroundings. Look for heavy draperies, carpeting, thickly upholstered seats, other objects which absorb sound. Clap your hands and listen for sound reverberation. The reverberation of the clap can tell quite a bit about the acoustics of a room.

With the variables involved in solo performance, there is one thing which is very predictable. The pressure and anxiety of public performance will cause the tempo to rush. If this rushing tendency is anticipated, adjustments can be made in the starting tempo so that the piece does not accelerate out of control. Once the various performance tempi have been set, the player should make note of the metronome markings and return and check these periodically to be sure the practical limits have not been passed.

The same rushing tendency occurs when reviewing orchestral excerpts in preparation for an audition. As the excerpts are performed more and more, the tempi invariably begin to accelerate. This increase is so gradual that it is usually imperceptible to the player. It should therefore be understood that listening to recordings of the excerpts is not merely for initial learning. They are used for comparison throughout the audition preparation.

Part of the physical preparation for a performance should include previewing the material before the actual contest. The preview can be done before friends, family, or by performing the program at another location and it should be scheduled enough in advance of the contest so that appropriate adjustments can be made where necessary. The preview performance should be kept informal so that the atmosphere remains as relaxed as possible.

Mental Preparation

It is easier to say that a positive mental attitude should be maintained than it is to create such an outlook. The soloist must not see the audience as an adversary. The audience wants the performer to do his best and to feel comfortable.

The first step to creating this attitude is to develop a secure knowledge of the material. It is helpful sometimes to have the student memorize the material, even if this is not required for the performance. Memorizing tends to make one overlearn, so that confidence is greater.

The performer should try to create the performance environment prior to the actual presentation. Imagining the presence of an audience, the sound of applause, the lights, etc., helps the soloist retain composure when he is actually under those conditions. He might even wear more formal clothing when practicing, and duplicate as much of the general atmosphere as possible.

When an abundance of preparation has gone into a contest, part of the actual performance is turned over to the subconscious. Thinking of all the previously mastered technical details during a performance can actually be a distraction. Examples of this mental attitude can be found in W. Timothy Gallwey's *The Inner Game of Tennis.* One case tells of a student who is preoccupied with the mechanics of the tennis swing. Invariably, after a few volleys the ball is hit into the net. When the direction of thought was changed to an awareness of smooth strokes, the volleys continue indefinitely. This concept also applies to the musician. When his mind is no longer preoccupied with the execution of technical elements, the complete musical ideas will be conveyed to the audience.

The student should think of himself in the role of a successful performer. If he is playing a solo on the piccolo trumpet, he could see himself as Maurice André or Armando Ghitalla. The concept of role playing is described in *An Actor Prepares,* by Constantine Stanislavski.

An excellent book on the positive function of the mind is *Psychocybernetics* by Maxwell Maltz. Dr. Maltz sees the self image as the key to human personality and behavior. Personality and behavior cannot be changed until the self image is changed. When the self image is assured the student is likely to have positive musical experiences.

The Performance

The performer should attempt to remain at ease as much as possible prior to the performance. After a schedule for the day is established and the warm-up time is set, he should make an effort to keep his mind off the contest itself. Many people find reading a book sufficient to keep their thoughts occupied.

When the performance time arrives, walk out on the stage in a business-like manner, being sure to take calm, relaxed breaths. Awareness of the breathing will help retain composure. Walk quickly enough to reach the playing position on stage before the applause dies away. This means one does not walk too briskly, but at the same time it cannot be a leisurely stroll.

After the accompanist has arrived at the piano, the audience's applause is acknowledged with a bow. A bow is not merely a nod of the head, but a relaxed bend at the waist.

After the applause dies away, tune carefully. It is a good idea to check intonation with the piano before the concert, so the pre-performance tuning is merely a double-check. If in the anxiety of the moment it is impossible to ascertain whether you are flat or sharp, the best solution is to pull the tuning slide out further than necessary and work up to the pitch. Flatness in pitch is much easier to recognize than sharpness. The soloist sounds the pre-determined tuning pitch first, stops the sound, and the same pitch is played on the piano. Any other tuning adjustment is done similarly with the soloist and accompanist playing the pitches one after the other. It is easier to hear pitch discrepancies when the notes are sounded individually.

If the pitch changes during the performance, invariably it will become sharp, so it may be necessary to pull out the slide at a rest point.

After the tuning is established, there should be enough of a pause to let the audience settle and the accompanist prepare. During this time the soloist collects his thoughts and directs his attention to the opening music of the composition. If the piece begins with accompaniment alone the soloist gives a slight nod in the direction of the accompanist when he is ready to begin.

If there is a tendency to shake, the performer should concentrate on relaxing the neck, back and shoulders while breathing deeply. The legs should remain relaxed and the knees flexible. There should never be the feeling that the feet are anchored in place on the floor.

A common problem with some brass players is the feeling that the mouth has become completely dry. This is caused by a lack of saliva flow. Many performers will take a glass of water on stage with them. Sometimes it is not necessary to use it, but just the presence of it is reassuring enough to keep the saliva flowing. Others find that drinking water will wash away the remaining saliva and only compound the problem. Each person should know his own system well enough to predict what the response will be. The water should never be colder than room temperature or the lips will be chilled. The flow of saliva can often be stimulated by lightly biting the sides of the tongue or rubbing the tongue in the bottom of the mouth.

It will be necessary during the course of the solo to empty the condensation from the instrument. Release the condensation during the piano interludes, but do it as discretely as possible. Blowing through the instrument violently or shaking the instrument excessively will distract from the accompanist who is the principal performer at that time.

If it becomes necessary to wipe away perspiration, this should be done during a pause between movements. If it is essential to do it during a movement, the soloist can turn away from the audience and wipe the face with a folded handkerchief.

When the performer is confident of his preparation, is able to control nervous tendencies, can maintain complete attention to the solo, and has a sincere enjoyment of what he is trying to do, this security will be transmitted to the audience. As mentioned before in this section, the audience is hopeful for as successful a performance as possible.

Performance After a Wait

Unusual problems exist when there is a long wait before a solo or audition. This may occur in a variety of circumstances for the trumpet player, but the method of preparation is basically the same for all. One of the more difficult situations occurs in the performance of G. F. Handel's *Messiah*. If the complete version is performed it is not unusual to wait on stage as long as 45 minutes before the trumpet obbligato in the bass aria, "The Trumpet Shall Sound." Long waits are also not uncommon at auditions and in church services.

During these long periods, attention to the music should be sustained, but without becoming preoccupied with whatever difficulties are involved. Again, if there has been adequate preparation, the difficulties should be minimal. Some of the physical adjustments necessary would be to warm the instrument to temperature by blowing air through the trumpet a few minutes before starting. The mouthpiece should be warmed in the hands so that it doesn't chill the lips. The mouthpiece can then be placed on the lips to re-accustom the player to the embouchure position.

After the Performance

At the conclusion of a solo performance the soloist should bow to acknowledge the applause of the audience. At this time it is proper to also recognize the accompanist by asking him to stand and bow. Coordination of this activity will enhance the overall presentation. The performer and accompanist should take one or two bows and exit immediately. After leaving the stage, if the applause continues, the individuals should return together after a few seconds to take another bow. An exception to this might be following the last selection of a recital where one performer has been the featured soloist throughout the program. In this case the soloist alone would return for another bow.

Second and possible third bows should not be taken from the position on the stage where the performance was given. It is only necessary to go part way onto the stage. This avoids causing any embarassment to either the audience or performer by having to prolong the applause. The entrance and exit will be much quicker this way.

At the end of an orchestral audition or adjudication session there is usually no applause. The performer will merely exit from the stage or room when the presentation is finished.

Etiquette

If the soloist and accompanist are both male or both female, there are no problems with stage etiquette. The soloist enters first and, depending on the position of the piano, the soloist can either lead or follow the accompanist on departure. On second bows, which are close to the exit, the soloist can lead the entrance and the accompanist can lead the exit thus avoiding the problems of who leaves first and whether one person crosses in front of the other. More commonly, the soloist always leads on the first exit, and crosses in front of the accompanist to exit after a second bow.

When the soloist is female and the accompanist is male, the pianist will always follow, and on second bows he must stand so that the soloist can cross in front of him when she departs. He should take care not to stand in her way as she attempts to exit.

When the soloist is male and the pianist is female, the rules are changed. The pianist enters and departs first. On second bows, the soloist can lead the pianist on by the hand, but this would be the only circumstance where the soloist would precede the pianist. Otherwise, the accompanist enters ahead of the soloist, and crosses in front of him to lead the departure. The soloist should rehearse all stage action beforehand with someone in the audience to criticize the action and offer advice. The action should be rehearsed for speed and in concert dress, particularly with a male soloist and a female pianist. High heels and a narrow formal dress could greatly slow the speed that was rehearsed with a street dress and moderate heels. The female pianist should move with her greatest speed and grace so that the applause will not be wasted on labored entrances and departures.

The page turner is invisible by present day concert manners. He or she enters last, departs last and moves as inconspicuously as possible.

Chapter 21
Concert Deportment in Ensembles

The act of taking coordinated bows in a chamber music group generally will be determined by the number in the ensemble. Usually if there is no conductor, the ensemble will bow together. It is helpful to determine where each one will stand upon rising so that no person is blocked from the view of the audience. When all reach their positions, the bows are cued by a player who is visible to the entire group.

The stage deportment of the players in a large ensemble is just as important as that of the more visible players in a small ensemble. Although often ignored by most of the audience, there have been times when poor deportment has led to the firing of a player. Particularly in highly competitive positions, no deviation from proper deportment is tolerated. Notice how still both television and symphony orchestra players remain while resting during or between pieces. Their posture is not rigid in a military way, but they remain motionless with their heads and eyes facing forward. Just as you do not flourish a towel or handkerchief in a solo recital, you do not withdraw and replace music in the folder in a way that distracts the audience and breaks the mood. Many amateur groups forget the conductor and the audience when one number is completed, and they begin preparing for the next composition. They return one piece and remove the next piece from the folder while the conductor attempts to acknowledge the applause. This music change looks like a flock of white-winged birds about to take off. The mood of the concert is further ruined when the conductor attempts to have the group stand to accept some of the applause. As they are not paying attention, they are not aware of the request to stand and they get to their feet one by one rather than as a group.

A professional group is attentive to the conductor and the audience during applause. If the music for the next part of the program must be prepared, it is removed from the folder by curling it so that it is not seen by the audience. The movement of the arms, head and torso are restricted so that there is no illusion of movement, and the conductor is watched so that should they be asked to rise they can do so as a group. This standing and sitting is usually controlled by the concertmaster (or a solo woodwind player in a wind ensemble), and the group stands when he stands and sits when he sits. Should the conductor enter from the wings and gesture for the group to rise without going to the podium, another person should indicate to the concertmaster that the signal to stand has been given. The group should not sit again until the conductor has left the stage, and as the concertmaster cannot see this either, the principal cellist usually gives him a cue.

The trumpeter may have the feeling that as he is seated in or near the back row he is not seen and therefore the rules of deportment do not apply to him. The deportment is the same whether it is a solo recital or a large symphony orchestra. Members of the audience have good eyesight and some have expensive binoculars. One of these persons may be the manager or the conductor's wife. The trumpet players must remain attentive even during *tacit* movements of a long symphony. Their eyes and heads must face forward, and if they must exchange information such as what the count of a long rest is, it must be whispered through still lips while looking straight ahead or signalled with the hands or fingers which are resting on the thighs well below the line of sight of even the highest seat in the balcony.

The basis of deportment is a respect for music, a respect for the conductor and a respect for the audience. Everyone benefits when nothing is done to distract from the performance. Most decisions regarding deportment which have not been discussed in this chapter, can be solved logically if the respect for and mutual appreciation of music are considered first and foremost by all concerned.

Chapter 22

Selecting the Appropriate Instrument

Trumpet performers have the unique opportunity of selecting from a variety of differently pitched instruments to produce the tone quality they feel is appropriate in various compositions. This chapter is written to give some insights that can be used for making that selection.

Players welcome the opportunity to create different fingering patterns by changing to an instrument of another key. Many experienced professionals believe that the way a passage "lays under the fingers" is the primary reason for selecting an instrument of a particular key, and they consider tone quality second. Notice how the fingering difficulty of the following passages varies with the instrument selected.

Stravinsky, "Danse Infernale" from *The Firebird* as written:

alternate possibility:

102

Prokofiev, *Lieutenant Kije* as written:

alternate possibility:

Tschaikovsky, *Symphony No. 4* as written:

alternate possibility:

Tschaikovsky, *Capriccio Italien* as written:

alternate possibility:

Stravinsky, *Le Sacre du Printemps* as written:

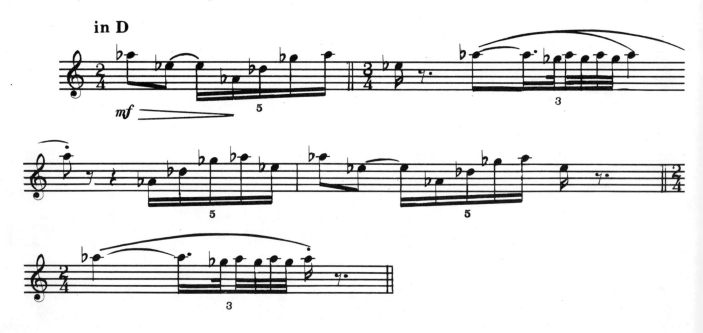

alternate possibility:

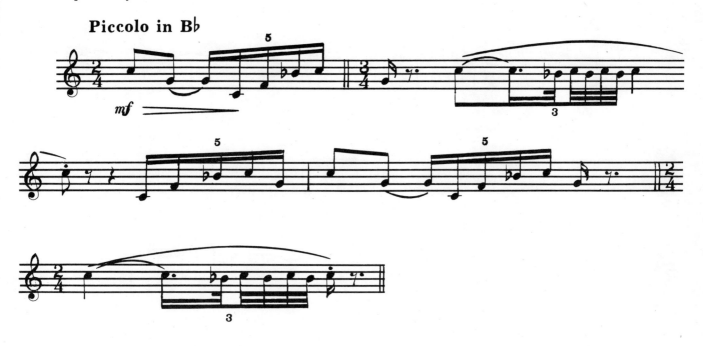

Stravinsky, *Petrouchka* as written:

alternate possibility:

Ravel, *Alborada del Gracioso* as written:

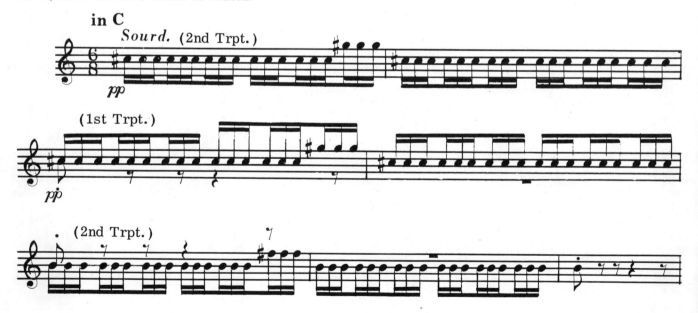

alternate possibility:

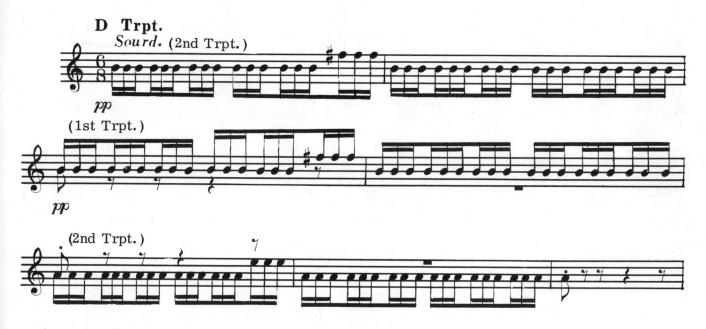

Mahler, *Symphony No. 3* as written:

alternate possibility:

Wagner, Prelude to *Parsifal* as written:

in F

alternate possibility:

E♭ Trpt.

Bartok, *Concerto for Orchestra* as written:

alternate possibility:

Stravinsky, *Pulcinella* as written:

alternate possibility:

Ravel, *Bolero* as written:

alternate possibility:

Mussorgsky-Ravel, "Samuel Goldenberg and Schmuyle" from *Pictures at an Exhibition* as written:

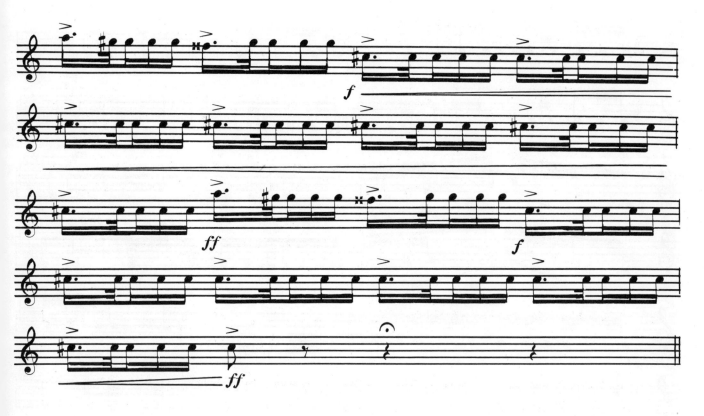

alternate possibility:

A Piccolo Trpt.

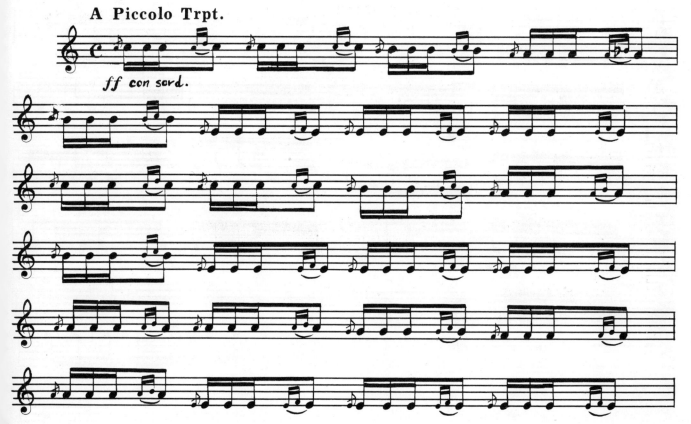

It is my belief that *most* composers do not write their music with a specific tone quality in mind. Granted, they are aware of the generally accepted tone of the instrument in their country during their era, the ability to alter that tone by using mutes, and the scoring and technical limitations of the instrument, but if asked to describe the tone difference between B flat, C, and D trumpets, many would have difficulty providing a meaningful answer. If their compositions are played accurately and with the appropriate musical style, they usually will be pleased with the effect.

This fact is less true with conductors. They usually have a more specific idea as to the tone color they prefer. The trumpeter is fortunate, however, because the wide variety of bore and bell sizes throughout the various pitched trumpets gives the player the latitude to select an instrument which has a tone color that will satisfy the conductor and yet is in a key that allows the performer to feel secure with the fingering combinations in the various passages.

The list below illustrates several examples of orchestral repertoire having prominent trumpet parts. Many of these would be recognized as *standard repertoire* in that they are frequently performed and are often specified as requirements for orchestral auditions. The first column gives the written key for the trumpet part. The second lists the pitch of the trumpet often used on all or part of the composition. Naturally this choice is arbitrary and these should be recognized only as suggestions worth considering. I make no pretense of giving a complete list. A complete list would be a task worthy of an entire book. It should also be noted that the C trumpet is the instrument used most often by orchestral players today. I have not bothered to give examples where that would be the obvious choice.

	written for trumpet in:	possible alternate choice
Bach, J. S., *B Minor Mass*	D	piccolo A
Brandenburg Concerto	F	piccolo B flat or piccolo C
Christmas Oratorio	D	piccolo A
Magnificat	D	piccolo A
Suites No. 3 and 4	D	piccolo A
Beethoven, *Consecration of the House*	C	D
Copland, *El Salon Mexico*	C	D
Handel, *Judas Maccabaeus*	D	piccolo A
Messiah	D	piccolo A
Royal Fireworks Music	D	piccolo A
Samson	D	piccolo A
Water Music	D	piccolo A
Hindemith, *Mathis der Maler*	C	D
Koldáy, *Hary-Janos Suite* (cornet part in the Fifth Movement)	B flat	E flat
Prokofiev, *Scythian Suite* (Ala and Lolly)	E flat	piccolo B flat
Ravel, *Piano Concerto*	C	D
Respighi, *Pines of Rome* (off-stage solo)	C	D
Rimsky-Korsakoff, *Russian Easter Overture*	B flat and A	D
Stravinsky, *Petrouchka* (Ballerina's Dance)	B flat	E flat

Chapter 23
The Professional Attitude

The subject of this chapter is by no means limited to individuals who are professionals strictly because by definition music is the way they make their livelihood. Students should begin to cultivate this attitude early in their musical studies or they will never achieve the status of professionals in the literal sense of the word.

Students with sincere musical aspirations must be highly motivated and totally dedicated to their work. This incentive certainly should not be to the point of obsession or missing out on the true meaning of life, but it is essential that music have a high priority. The rationale and motivation for practicing a musical instrument is often difficult to understand, particularly in a multi-disciplinary academic situation where other students may not need the same degree of determination.

There are several other aspects of one's musical life which must be established as routine. While all of these are mundane to some extent, they must be accepted as part of the business as a whole. The mature musician in an organization knows the relevance of his part to the musical score, counts measures rest, works for good section intonation (even if it means admitting his own intonation might not always be the most appropriate) and is responsible so his colleagues know they can count on him for musical accuracy.

It is imperative to develop the ability to concentrate. There are very few instances, particularly in large ensembles, where the trumpeters play continuously. They must condition themselves not to allow mental lapses during the times when playing demands are less. Most people are not able to maintain intense concentration for anything more than a short period of time. Musicians in their practicing should strive to maintain this continuity, regardless of how mundane and routine the material might be. In this way they will develop the habit of mentally repressing any thoughts which are not relevant to their performing. There will be instances of distraction even in concert performances. Experienced musicians will not let a missed note or incorrect entrance interrupt their thinking. Losing control of their concentration is only inviting situations where errors begin to pile one on another and lead to the inevitable disaster. Once this degree of concentration is developed, it is maintained at the same level, regardless of the difficulty of the composition.

A Haydn symphony is not approached with any less care than a Strauss tone poem, although an immature player may think the Haydn is easier.

Musicians, because of the unique qualifications for their work, must possess artistic sensitivity. They often have sensitive feelings about their work as well. Mature musicians, both student and professional, should keep this in mind in their relationships with colleagues. It is professionally irresponsible to practice another player's solo passages in his presence, to distract others with conversation when you know their utmost concentration must be on their work, to stare at them when they are trying to play a difficult passage, or to make comments on their work when you know (as obviously they know) they have not played their best.

Musicians are called upon for a higher degree of cooperation than many other professions. Their work is truly a team effort. In day-to-day schedules this necessitates that each individual put forth his best effort for the success of the whole organization. Cooperation is further tested when an ensemble is on tour. Continuous proximity of different personalities, playing in a strange (usually inferior) environment, and irregular eating and sleeping routines all test an individual's ability to cooperate. Regardless of these things, every person is expected to put forth his best effort for success of the organization.

Well-trained musicians often have creative ideas which they feel will enhance the music that is being performed. How much of this creativity may be exercised varies greatly. In a solo recital the performer may make all of the artistic decisions. With a chamber music group there is usually an interchange of ideas until a conclusion is reached which satisfies the majority. There is much less freedom, however, in a large ensemble, where the ideas and decisions of the conductor prevail. While the opportunity for original expression may vary with each conductor, the players must be prepared to understand that once a decision is made, like it or not, they are responsible for performing with that musical interpretation.

At what stage in a musician's development does one achieve this mysterious professional attitude? The answer is not simple—sometimes early, sometimes never. Many students will come by it naturally. Others can learn by having someone detail the ideas to them. Those who are never able to comprehend will face untold frustration and disappointment.

Chapter 24
Developing Musical Style

The contemporary music student represents a curious combination of innate ability which is often called *natural,* techniques which are developed by formal training, and judgments which are cultivated by musical experience.

Nothing is more overworked than the idea that successful performers have risen to that echelon because they have come by it *naturally*. There are scores of cases which illustrate the continuity of famous musical performers through generations of a family. It would be impossible to determine how much of this continuity was attributable to heredity and how much environment was responsible. Continuous exposure to fine music through recordings, concert attendance, and parental supervision and encouragement, are all too often lumped into the category which people hastily will refer to as natural ability. There is no doubt that some individuals are blessed with more talent resources than others. Witness students who have pitch recognition contrasted with those who are unable to match a note to say nothing of having the note in tune, or those who can duplicate intricate rhythms with those who cannot clap four equal beats. It is still necessary for the gifted students to practice countless hours to reach their full level of ability development.

An individual performs music by reading symbols (notes, rests, dynamics, expression marks, tempo indications) from the printed page, transferring these to sounds because he possesses technical command of an instrument, adding a knowledge of history and composer's style, and finally by exercising musical taste and judgment. When all of these factors are used competently, a stylistically correct musical performance is created. Too many students are content with only the symbol reading and technical performance. The other factors are what truly give music its style and flavor.

An awareness of both world history and music history are necessary to perform music satisfactorily. Events in history and the condition of society have always had an influence on musical composition and performance. In addition to this, performers must be aware of interpretation and stylistic trends during various periods in the growth and development of music. How can we expect to correctly interpret the music of Haydn, Hindemith or any composer without a knowledge of the composer, his life, and his environment?

Musical taste and judgment relate to the interpretation of the variables within the printed symbols. What is the appropriate dynamic change in a *crescendo?* Is the printed *ritard* to be played in an exaggerated style or should it be interpreted conservatively? These and hundreds of other judgments face the performer constantly. At the same time, he must make judgments regarding appropriate musical phrasing. Although phrasing must be decided in an analytical way, the overall effect must be to enhance the music.

The existence of musical style provides the difference between a colorless interpretation of the printed page and one which is vibrant and alive. An analogy would be the boredom suffered when listening to a speaker using no inflection in the voice. It would be difficult to maintain interest long enough to have any idea of the message. The same is often true in musical performance.

Young students should be able to draw ideas in tastefully correct interpretation from exposure to a good teacher and by attentively listening to professional performers in concerts and on recordings.

It is sad to see young musicians who have learned the notes of a musical composition and have mastered all the technical passages, who feel at that point that they have mastered the piece. These students do not realize they have come to know the composition by taking the steps to learning it in reverse order. The proper sequence is first to determine the composer's intention and the musical concept, then to learn the notes within that conceptual framework.

Chapter 25

Mutes

Using mutes provides an infinite variety of tone colors when trumpets and cornets are played either as a solo instrument or in a section. This change of tone quality is the primary function of mutes. Most mutes soften the volume of tone in addition to altering timbre; however, this dynamic change is not the specific reason for muting a passage.

It is important to be familiar with the playing properties of the various mutes. In addition to changing the timbre of the instrument, they also create problems by changing the blowing properties and the intonation of the instrument. Since all of these qualities vary with each type of mute, they are discussed separately.

A director who is striving for absolute uniformity of quality from each type of mute might wish to see that students purchase a similar brand, since there is even some discrepancy in tone color between the products of different manufacturers. This need for uniformity is particularly true in stage bands where the smaller number of players in the ensemble make this timbre discrepancy more apparent.

There are literally dozens of trumpet and cornet mutes available. However, most of these are variations to some degree on four basic types mutes—the straight mute, the cup mute, the wa-wa or Harmon mute, and the plunger. The following discussion of the functions of these mutes, plus a few usable exceptions, will provide a comprehensive view as to their practical application.

Straight Mute—Metal

The most common type of mute is the straight mute. Whenever a mute is designated in a musical score with no specific instructions as to the type, it should be assumed a straight mute is implied. A chart showing the various foreign terminology for muting is included at the end of this section.

The metal straight mute is made of spun aluminum; however, some manufacturers will include models with copper or brass ends to achieve a slightly different timbre. It gives the trumpet or cornet a tone which varies from a slight buzz at a soft dynamic to a brittle rasp at a *forte*. The tone quality of a metal straight mute sometimes gives the impression that the instrument is being played louder than is actually the case.

The metal straight mute often raises the pitch of the instrument slightly. It then becomes necessary to pull out the tuning slide a fraction of an inch when using the mute.

The fit of the metal straight mute in the bell of the instrument is very critical. The mutes generally come with thicker corks than are needed. This extra thickness allows for the adjustment to individual bell sizes. These corks can easily be lowered to the proper height with coarse sandpaper. The way to determine the correct height is to play the mute in the low register of the instrument. A mute which has too much cork will be stuffy to play in the range around the low A flat, G, and G flat. The resulting tone will have a foggy, uncentered quality. Each cork should be *gradually* sanded an equal amount. Test the mute in the instrument frequently. As you get close to the correct amount of cork, these notes will begin to come into focus. Stop sanding when the tone of those three notes matches the quality of the notes in the staff. Take care to remove only the minimum amount necessary. If excessive cork is sanded away, the pitch will be raised excessively.

Fig. 58 Straight Mutes (left to right: cardboard, hardboard, plastic, aluminum, and aluminum piccolo trumpet straight mute)

Straight Mute—Fiber

Straight mutes also may be constructed of fiber board or cardboard. These were popular before developments in the metal straight mutes improved their quality and lowered the price. They have retained their popular

120

appeal because the price is still about one-half that of the metal straight mute. The fiber straight mute has a less raspy quality than the metal mute. They are especially effective in an extremely soft passage where the straight mute quality is still desired. It is not common to designate in a musical score whether a metal or fiber straight mute is intended. Intonation deficiencies are similar to the metal straight mute.

Straight Mute—Plastic

A third type of straight mute, one made of plastic, has come on the market in recent years. Its low price has made it appealing to many trumpet students, but I do not encourage the plastic mute for two reasons. First, the outer surface is so smooth it is difficult to get the corks to adhere. After very little use the cork may slip into the wrong position or fall off. Second, the mute will crack if it is dropped. A crack or chip in one of these plastic mutes is almost impossible to repair.

Cup Mute

Cup mutes are used extensively in dance bands, combos, and commercial work. They are rarely used in symphony orchestras. The corks on a cup mute often need to be filed. The normal intonation idiosyncrasies with cup mutes are the opposite of the straight mute. Most cup mutes make the pitch *flat,* so it is necessary to push the tuning slide in a little. The cup mute produces a softer, more resonant tone than the straight mute. Scores will specify *cup mute* or *sourdine bol* when its use is intended.

Fig. 59 Other Mutes (left to right: rubber plunger, bucket Charlie Spivak "Wispa" mute, and Solotone)

Wa-Wa or Harmon

The wa-wa mute is used for numerous effects in jazz playing. Its use in symphonic literature is limited to a few isolated examples, Gershwin's *Rhapsody in Blue* being one of the better known illustrations. The wa-wa mute can be used to produce a variety of tone colors by adjusting the position of the stem. With the stem in all the way it has a timbre with the resonance of the cup mute, but a soft raspiness. Pulling the stem out gradually makes this timbre become softer and softer. When the stem is removed the raspiness disappears completely, but the dynamic is a little louder than with the stem extended.

The wa-wa mute derives its name from the ability to produce that effect by alternately covering and removing the hand from over the stem. This is indicated in the musical score with a + sign for the hand closing and an o for the hand removed.

The score may designate wa-wa or Harmon mute. Harmon is a trade name but there are several other manufacturers who produce wa-wa mutes which serve the same function.

Fig. 60 Wa-Wa or Harmon Mute

One hazard in using a wa-wa mute is having it fall out of the instrument. The back pressure created by the mute makes even a new mute with good cork susceptible to this problem. There are two solutions to this. A small amount of powdered rosin can be put on the cork. Be careful not to use too much or the mute will squeak when it is removed from the bell.

Blowing a puff of warm air inside the bell will also help the mute to stay in securely. This forms a thin layer of water vapor on the metal surface and increases the adhesion of the cork.

Fig. 61 Blowing Air into the Bell

Plunger

Mute manufacturers make a plunger mute, but an acceptable (and more popular) substitute is what is commonly known as a "plumber's friend." These are available in a variety of sizes from any store selling plumbing equipment. The small size which is generally used to open clogged sinks is appropriate for the trumpet bell.

The notation for using the plunger is the same as the wa-wa mute—+ for the bell covered and o for the bell open. It is also possible to create any number of unusual effects by partially covering the bell or varying the speed of the opening and closing.

Hat, Metal Hat, or Derby

The hat mute is used mainly to duplicate the sound from the big band era. It is slightly elliptically shaped, measuring six and one-half by eight inches on the inside and is about four inches deep. The same size hat mute is used for both trumpet and trombone. It is mounted on a stand and the bell of the trumpet is pointed into the hat. The amount of timbre adjustment will vary with the depth of the bell into the hat. The hat may also be removed from the stand and held over the bell with the left hand. The hand may then open and close the bell with the hat or pass it across the end of the bell.

Felt Hat

The felt hat is used to give a covered, dampened sound to the trumpet tone. There is an extended trumpet

Fig. 62 Hat, Metal Hat, or Derby Mute

solo played into a "felt crown" in the second movement of George Gershwin's *Concerto in F* for piano and orchestra. It also may be used for special effects by jazz trumpeters playing solos into a microphone.

A felt hat mute can be made by cutting the top out of an old hat. Then cut a slit about two inches long about one inch in from the edge of the crown. The slit then fits over the rim of the bell.

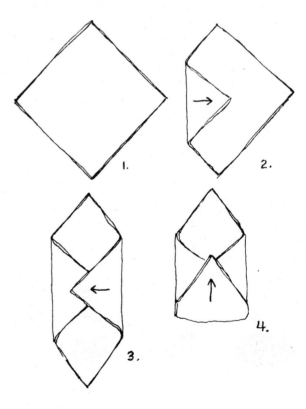

Fig. 63 Folding Felt Envelope Mute

Another way to make a felt crown mute is to cut a piece of felt material in the shape of a disassembled envelope. The felt envelope is then folded and sewn or glued together with one flap left open. The envelope then hangs inverted over the rim of the bell with the back side and the flap covering the end of the bell. The envelope should be constructed so that it hangs loosely over the bell. If it fits too tightly, it will affect the pitch and dampen the sound too much.

Fig. 64 Felt Envelope Mute over Trumpet Bell

Charlie Spivak "Whispa Mute"

The Whispa Mute has a cork completely around the end to seal it into the bell. All the sound from the instrument is directed into the mute. There is a non-movable hollow tube inside and a cap covering the end with felt dampers between the cap and the body of the mute. This produces the softest dynamic of all the trumpet mutes.

In symphony orchestra playing it may be used by the three trumpets to simulate the distant call in Claude Debussy's "Fetes" from *Three Nocturnes*. It is also a handy mute to use in hotels for warming up or quiet practice.

Solotone Mute

The *Solotone* mute looks something like a straight mute with a portion of another straight mute attached to the end. It differs in that it has cork completely around the end to seal the mute into the bell and a hole from the first chamber of the mute into the second chamber. The second acts as a megaphone for the sound and focuses the tone.

The solotone mute is used nowadays in solo jazz combo work. It is particularly effective when played into a microphone.

Bucket

The bucket mute is a large cannister with an open end which faces the bell of the instrument. The cannister is filled with a soft, sound absorbing material and the whole unit is attached to the bell of the trumpet by three spring clips. This suspends the whole unit about an inch away from the end of the bell. The bucket gives a very interesting soft, covered tone.

Mutes for the Higher Key Trumpets

There are straight mutes and wa-wa mutes available for the unusually small bell of the piccolo A-B flat trumpets. The straight mute is used in some orchestral repertoire, the wa-wa mute in commercial jingles and for quiet practice. In the case of the D-E flat instrument and the F-G instrument, mutes for the *mezzo-soprano* trumpet can be adapted to fit by filing the corks. Carefully examine the flair at the throat of the bell so the corks can be filed exactly as needed. It may be necessary to shape the contour of the corks as well as lower them.

Chart of mute terminology

English	mute	with mute	open without mute
French	Sourdine (Sourd.)	Avec Sourdine Mettre la Sourdine	Sans Sourdine Enlevez la Sourdine Otez la Sourdine
Italian	Sordina Sordino (Sord.)	Con Sordina Mettere Sordina	Senza Sordina Via Sordina Sordina levata
German	Dämpfer	Mit Dämpfer	Ohne Dämpfer Dämpferweg

Chapter 26
Contemporary Techniques

Every historical period in music has had performance techniques which could be considered innovative and difficult. Composers have always sought to both use and expand the performance potential of players and their instruments to the fullest. The present age in music is no exception to this. Perhaps it is because we have the opportunity of witnessing the implementation of these techniques that many players feel the demands presently made of the trumpet performer are the highest expectations which have ever existed. One of the reasons for this is that the opportunity for technical development invariably follows the necessity for implementation. This sequence puts the performer in the awkward position of mastering only those techniques which are thrust upon him for a specific composition. The object of this chapter is to discuss in a general way some of the techniques which are expected of trumpet performers by contemporary composers and present a plan by which students can learn to develop these techniques before they are required to use them.

Some players feel that contemporary music is less demanding because they may take more liberties. This may be true in some of the aleatory or chance music, where many things are left to the performer's imagination. In a sense, the performer is creating a composition with each playing of the work as his ideas are combined with those of the composer. While it might seem that this would allow considerable freedom within approximate guidelines, it is still necessary for the performer to have a knowledge of the composer's style and to have improvisational ability within that style. In reality, most music composed today requires a keen sense of rhythmic and pitch accuracy which at least equals, if not surpasses, any demands which have been made previously on performers.

Two books which help students think in meters other than the conventional $\frac{2}{4}$, $\frac{3}{4}$, $\frac{4}{4}$, and $\frac{6}{8}$ are *Odd Meter Duets* and *Odd Meter Etudes,* by Everett Gates. While these are not technically challenging to many students beyond the high school level, they serve to break the conventional mold of symmetry within measures of music. Robert Nagel's *Trumpet Studies in Contemporary Music* is a useful follow-up to the Gates books. These explore more of a variety of problems than the Gates books and are technically more difficult. Studying a combination of these books should prepare students for the more advanced ideas of contemporary composers.

The intervallic relationships of today's music are often angular and dissonant. Verne Reynolds' *48 Etudes for Trumpet* is an excellent book for the development of the aural perception of the less familiar intervals. Although quite advanced technically, the book also includes some legato studies. Most trumpet students should have studied a wide variety of etude material before attempting these studies.

We need to be concerned with three main aspects of contemporary composition—rhythm, pitch, and sounds other than musical. It would be beneficial to briefly examine the scope of each of these beyond conventional compositional techniques.

Rhythmic Considerations

It is imperative that rhythmic figures be executed with exactness. In most cases odd multiples of notes are played with equal note value. Groups are not divided into two segments as is often done in more conventional music.

It is common to see the following rhythmic writing in contemporary music:

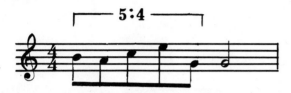

In this case the eighth notes are played in the following time span:

or another example:

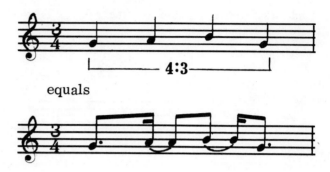

equals

In instances such as these, the numbers indicate the written number of notes to be played within the time usually allotted for the second number. All notes must be played with equal value.

Another common form of rhythmic writing is spatial notation (or proportional notation). The note values are generally represented by the distance between notes.

or another example:

Notes within an *accelerando* are usually written:

Notes in a decelerating sequence are indicated as:

Composers today also use a device called a time line. A given number of seconds (″) or minutes (′) is indicated above a figure and the passage is used to fill that amount of time.

Performers of contemporary music must be prepared to work with a stop watch, particularly in compositions which include recorded tapes. Passages such as extended time lines may be included, as well as interludes during which the tape plays by itself and the performer is required to wait for an indicated length of time. When working with tape, performers should be familiar enough with the tape to find specific cues to coordinate their part. Familiarity with the tape will allow performers to feel confident with their relationship within context of the complete composition.

Pitch Considerations

Unconventional use of vibrato is quite common in contemporary music. The composer will dictate the speed and width of the vibrato with notations such as:

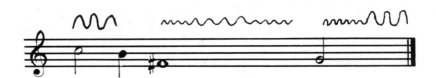

There are also instances when a composer asks for an absence of vibrato. They will usually notate this "no vibrato" or "N.V."

Many times indeterminate pitches will be noted. These will have stems to indicate rhythm, but an absence of note heads. Something should be played within the approximate range of the missing note head.

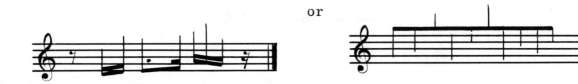

or

Another form of indeterminate pitch asks for the highest note possible or a series of high notes:

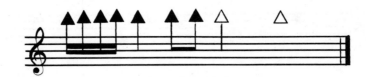

or the lowest note possible or series of low notes:

A *glissando* is noted:

Pitches may also be divided into quarter tones. These are noted for both quarter tones higher and lower.

Performers should work with their own instrument to find appropriate fingerings for quarter tones between each chromatic half step. These may be derived from alternate fingerings, by using the valve slides, or a combination of both of these. The following fingering chart will give some ideas as to possible quarter tone fingerings on various trumpets:

L. D. = Lip Down
⟶ = Slide Fully Extended
⟶⟶ = Slide Extended Half-Way

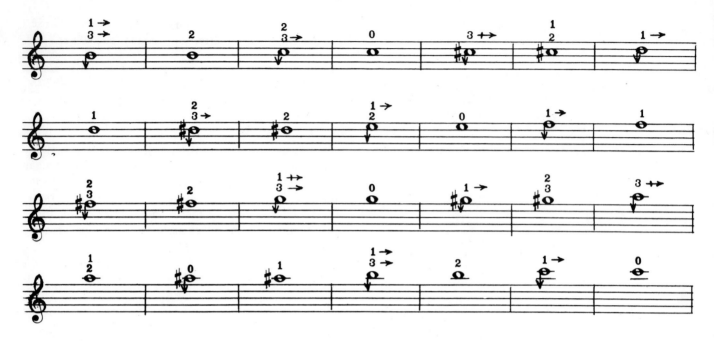

Composers may also write microtones which are pitch adjustments without the positive designation of quarter tones. These are normally indicated by an arrow which is not attached to the note.

Fig. 65 Half-Valve Technique

Notes may be written to be played with the valve depressed only part way. Although the technique is called half-valve and is usually indicated with $\frac{1}{2}$ over the notes, it is quite possible the valve will need to be lowered slightly more than half way to get the necessary effect. (See Fig. 65)

The performer may also be asked to sing or hum into the instrument while playing another note. This is usually indicated as:

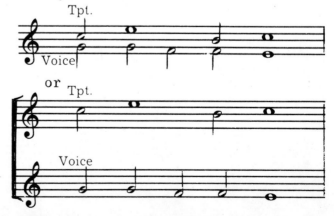

Unconventional Sounds

Composers make use of a myriad of sounds which do not fall within the scope of what would be considered tone production on the trumpet. Some of these include popping pitches by striking the mouthpiece, (both in and out of the instrument) with the palm of the hand, buzzing pitches on the mouthpiece alone, sucking air through the trumpet, kissing the mouthpiece, and clicking the valves.

Compositions which employ these unusual techniques will usually include a legend and explanatory notes to the performer stating the specific effect desired. Some have been in use long enough that their notation can be accepted as commonplace. A handy source for identifying some of these universally accepted forms is the *Notational Guide for Contemporary Trumpet,* published by Tromba Publications.

Two other valuable books for preparation and study of contemporary music are *Contemporary Trumpet Studies,* by Alfred Blatter, Paul Zonn and David Hickman, and *Contemporary Trumpet Studies,* by Thomas Stevens. A notational guide is included in the front of the Blatter, Zonn and Hickman book or it may be purchased separately. Trumpet players are fortunate to have these sources as study material prior to performing contemporary music.

Chapter 27
Fundamental Repair

Spending a few minutes informing students about instrument maintenance is time well invested. This could prevent expensive repair and the inconvenience of being without an instrument.

Cleaning the Mouthpiece

A special brush is available for cleaning the throat and backbore of the mouthpiece. Using the brush regularly with warm soapy water will prevent the build up of dirt and deposits. Washing also is essential for keeping the mouthpiece sanitary so that lip infections are prevented.

Students should be encouraged to use a mouthpiece brush as frequently as possible—every day it is hoped. Be sure the brush has a tightly wound wire stem and small bristles, otherwise the twisting motion will make the bristles fall out.

It is first inserted into the backbore, rotated, and then inserted into the throat from the opposite end of the mouthpiece. As a final step the rim and exterior are brushed.

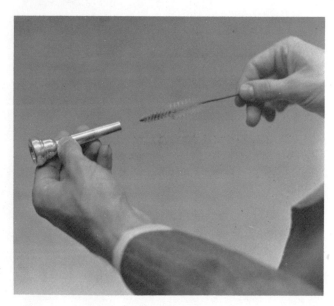

Fig. 66 Using the Mouthpiece Brush

Dents in the Mouthpiece

The end of the mouthpiece shank is quite thin and vulnerable to damage if it is dropped. A dent in this area can cause the mouthpiece to function improperly. Removing the dent is quite simple. Insert the end of a pair of needle-nose pliers into the backbore of the mouthpiece. When inserted to the point where the pliers come in contact with the dent, rotate them and keep pushing the pliers in gently as you rotate. Be careful not to expand the end of the shank beyond its original size or it will not fit into the mouthpiece receiver properly.

Fig. 67 Removing a Dent from the Mouthpiece Shank

Using the Cleaning Snake

The flexible snake is designed to clean the inside of the leadpipe and slides. It is a tightly wound spring with a brush on each end. The snake will pass around the large curves on a cornet or trumpet, but will not go completely through the valve slides.

If the snake is used regularly, (usually once a week), dirt and residue should get no further than the leadpipe and tuning slide. The tuning slide is removed and moderately warm water is rinsed through the leadpipe as the snake is inserted. Then the snake is passed through the tuning slide while running water through it. The snake is inserted in the direction of the air flow and pulled completely through.

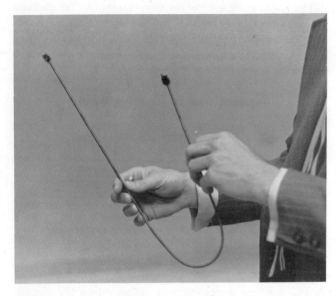

Fig. 68 Cleaning Snake

When rinsing the instrument the water should only be lukewarm. Hot water will make the lacquer blister and eventually peel off.

Valve Identification

Students should be shown how to properly identify the valves of the instrument. Each should have the number 1, 2, or 3 stamped on the spring casing or the base of the valve stem. This prevents them from becoming mixed up when all the valves are out at one time, as when cleaning.

Students also should know the correct position of the valve guides in the slots inside the cylinder. There is no universal way these guides are identified and this can create confusion. Some will have only one guide which inserts into a slot, some have two guides with one side larger than the other. The most confusing system is when both guides are the same size. Usually in this case, one will be identified with a mark, such as an X, so you can tell which side of the instrument it should face. (See Fig. 69 and Fig. 70)

It is a good idea for band directors to keep an inventory record for each school instrument in a loose leaf notebook. These inventory sheets would be a logical place to note how the valves for each cornet or trumpet are identified and how the guides fit into the slots inside the cylinder. These individual sheets on specific instruments can also be used to record repairs, rental fees, and list the names of the students to whom the instrument is signed out.

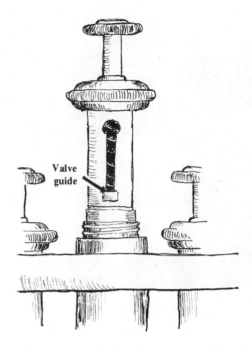

Fig. 69 Valve Guide

Fig. 70 Valve Cylinder Slots

Valve Maintenance

With proper care, trumpet valves should work satisfactorily for several years before any major maintenance is needed. The technique for oiling the valves is discussed in Chapter 1, "Handling the Trumpet."

Occassionally it will be necessary to remove the valves from the cylinders, wipe off the outside of the valves, and clean out the inside of the cylinders. This procedure is especially important with a new instrument because the valves are being lapped into the cylinders during the first few weeks of playing. During this lapping, a thin film of metal deposits is left on the surface of the valves. Premature wear will occur if these deposits remain on the valve surface.

Remove the valve and wipe it clean with a soft, lint-free cloth. (A one-foot square piece of double layered cheesecloth works quite well.) The valve is

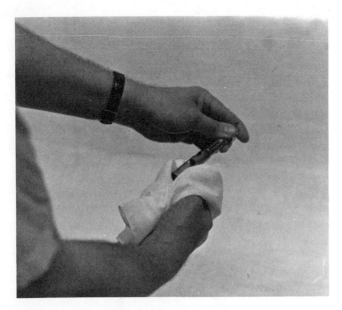

Fig. 71 Wiping the Valve

wiped by holding it on the index finger and applying a slight amount of pressure on the cloth with the thumb.

Remove the bottom valve cap and clean out any residue on the inside. Insert the cloth through the slot in a cleaning rod and push it through the inside of the cylinder to collect any oil or dirt. Be careful to push the rod straight through so the metal end does not come in contact with the walls of the cylinder. The bottom cap is replaced, the valve oiled and replaced in the cylinder.

The valves on a new instrument should be cleaned this way every day for the first few weeks. The process may be reduced to every other day and then to once a week when the amount of black residue on the valve begins to diminish.

Removing a Frozen Slide

Slides tend to become stuck when they are left in one position for a period of time. A small amount of corrosion forms around the end of the slide and makes it impossible to move. The tuning slide is least susceptible to this because it is adjusted each time the instrument is tuned. If it does become stuck, the following steps should be taken:

1. Run a few drops of penetrating oil down the leadpipe and let it pass down to the junction of the tuning slide.
2. Place a few drops of penetrating oil on the outside of the tuning slide where it goes into the leadpipe and lower sleeve. Allow a few minutes to let the oil penetrate.
3. Wrap a small, soft cloth (about the size of a hand towel) around the tuning slide and pull it out. If the slide refuses to loosen, you might try LIGHTLY tapping the outside of the slide with a rawhide mallet.

Fig. 72 Cleaning the Cylinder

Fig. 73 Removing a Frozen Tuning Slide

Valve slides are more apt to stick on students' instruments because they are moved less often. Their removal, although somewhat more difficult than the tuning slide, is well within the capability of any band director.

1. Place a few drops of penetrating oil at the junction of the slide and the sleeve.
2. Insert a wooden stick into the inner radius of the slide. A wooden drum stick with the tip removed is a good tool for this as the taper of the stick makes it fit various radii.
3. With the stick securely inserted into the inner curve of the slide and in perpendicular position, strike the side of the stick sharply with a rawhide hammer. Be sure the instrument is being held firmly.

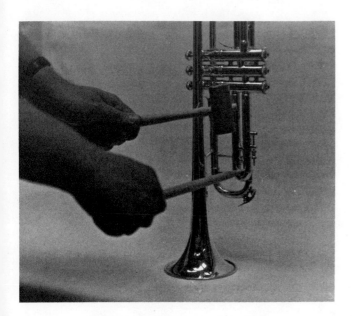

Fig. 74 Removing a Frozen Valve Slide

After any slide is loosened and removed, the inside should be cleaned with a snake. Oxidation which has collected on the outside sleeves of the slide may be removed with a *small* amount of brass polish or Lava soap. The slide is then lubricated with one of the commercially available slide greases or petroleum jelly and replaced in the instrument. When lubricating the slide, be careful not to get any grease on the inside of the slide.

Water Key Repair

Occasionally it is necessary to replace the spring or cork in the water key. The cork can be replaced without removing the water key from the instrument. The old cork is extracted with a small pen knife. Examine the cup into which the cork is inserted to be sure all traces of the cork have been removed. If any pieces remain, the new cork will not fit properly. Replacement corks are available in repair kits and from most music stores, but it may be necessary to sandpaper the cork since the size of the cup may be different on various makes of instruments. The cork should fit snugly into the cup. After checking the fit, the cork is removed and a small amount of contact cement is placed in the cup and on the cork, then the cork is replaced in the cup. Make sure there is no moisture on either the cup or the cork. The flat surface of the cork should cover the opening in the slide perfectly or there will be an air leak.

Most repair kits come with a variety of water key springs. Sometimes it is necessary to tailor one to fit specific needs, but this is not difficult. The screw which acts as an axis is removed, the new spring placed on the key, and the screw replaced. It is handy to have another person available to replace the screw, as the spring pressure sometimes makes alignment difficult. One person can hold the slide securely while the other lines up the water key and inserts the axis screw. The ends of the spring are usually longer than necessary and are removed with wire cutters after the spring is installed.

Using the Mouthpiece Puller

There are numerous brands of mouthpiece pullers, but every band director should own at least one. The

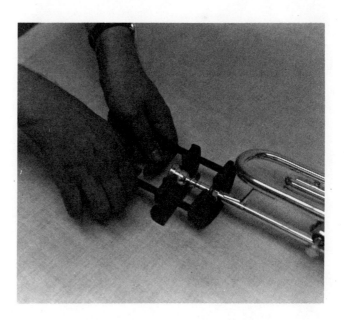

Fig. 75 Using the Mouthpiece Puller

puller in the illustration is the Thompson mouthpiece puller. It operates like a vise in reverse. There are several different size dies which insert into the puller. These vary in size to fit any mouthpiece shank from a French horn to a tuba. One of a pair of matching dies is inserted into the puller, the mouthpiece is placed with the junction of the shank and receiver at the die and the other die is placed in the puller. The two screws are then rotated clockwise to made the puller separate. Be sure to alternate sides and turn each handle a small amount (about half a turn). If you do not use this alternating sequence the puller may become jammed. Sometimes it is necessary to use pliers on the puller handles to get more leverage when a mouthpiece is particularly tight.

Pliers alone should never be used to remove a mouthpiece. The leadpipe braces are not strong enough to withstand this rotating and the leadpipe will be twisted in the process.

Realizing Limitations

While the band or orchestra director should not be reluctant to apply basic maintenance and repair techniques, he should also recognize there are limitations to what to try and repair. Work such as dents, misaligned slides, bent valve stems and other major repairs should be left for trained professionals.

Chapter 28
Selected Literature

Graded List of Literature and Technique

Level 1

Fundamentals of tone production, embouchure development and attack.

Typical Material:

Studies: Edwards-Hovey, *Method,* Book 1 (Belwin-Mills); S. Hering, *The Beginning Trumpeter,* (C. Fischer); J. Kinyon, *Breeze Easy Method,* Books 1 and 2 (M. Witmark).

Solos: J. Kinyon, *Breeze Easy Recital Pieces,* (Music Publishers Holding); Bach-Fitzgerald, *Bist du bei mir* (G. Ricordi); S. Lawton, *The Young Trumpet Player,* Vol. I (Oxford).

Technique: Major scales in G, C, F, B flat, E flat, A flat, and D flat, one octave, in quarter notes, M.M. quarter note = 72.

Level 2

Work in elementary legato style. Continued development of fundamentals.

Typical Material:

Studies: Edwards-Hovey, *Method,* Book 2 (Belwin); R. Getchell, *Practical Studies,* Books 1 and 2 (Belwin); S. Hering, *40 Progressive Etudes* (C. Fischer); L. Little, *Embouchure Builder* (Pro Art).

Solos: Teneglia-Fitzgerald, *Aria* (Theodore Presser); S. Lawton, *Young Trumpet Player* (Oxford).

Technique: All major scales and arpeggios, one octave, in eighth notes, M.M. quarter note = 72.

Level 3

Studies in tone control, breathing, flexibility, and articulation.

Typical Material:

Studies: S. Hering, *32 Etudes* (C. Fischer); C. Dalby, *Advanced Studies* (Belwin); Gower-Voxman, *Advanced Method,* Vol. 1 (Rubank).

Solos: B. Fitzgerald, *English Suite* (T. Presser);

Corelli-Powell, *Prelude and Minuet* (Southern); G. Balay, *Petite Piece Concertante* (Belwin).

Technique: All major scales and straight arpeggios, one or two octaves, in simple and compound rhythmic patterns, M.M. quarter note = 72.

Level 4

Further development of range, tone control, breathing, flexibility and articulation. Work on double and triple tonguing.

Typical Material:

Studies: H. Clark, *Technical Studies* (C. Fischer); H. Duhem, *24 Etudes* (Cundy-Bettoney); E. Gates, *Odd Meter Etudes* (D. Gornston); Concone-Sawyer, *Lyrical Studies* (Brass Press).

Solos: Bond-Finzi, *Concerto No. 1* (Boosey and Hawkes); Fiocco-Owen, *Arioso* (T. Presser); A. Petit, *Etude de concours* (Cundy-Bettoney); W. Eckard, *12 Program Solos* (T. Presser); Handel-Powell, *Sonata No. 3* (Southern).

Technique: All major and minor scales and straight arpeggios, one or two octaves, in simple and compound rhythmic patterns, M.M. quarter note = 72.

Level 5

A review of all the fundamentals of cornet and trumpet playing. Advanced flexibility exercises. Introduction to C, D, and A transpositions.

Typical Material:

Studies: E. F. Goldman, *Practical Studies* (C. Fisher); M. Schlossberg, *Daily Drills and Technical Studies* (M. Baron); H. Voxman, *Selected Studies* (Rubank); S. Hering, *The Orchestra Trumpeter* (C. Fischer).

Solos: A. Goedicke, *Concert Etude* (Leeds); Corelli-Fitzgerald, *Sonata VIII* (Ricordi); Gibbons-Cruft, *Suite* (J. Williams).

Technique: All major and minor scales, same as Level 4, plus diatonic pattern, all at M.M. quarter note = 84. Major and minor arpeggios in straight and broken form at M.M. = 72.

Level 6

Work with improvisation. Further development of range and flexibility. Addition of A flat, E flat, B, and F transpositions.

Typical Material:

Studies: H. L. Clark, *Characteristic Studies* (C. Fischer); P. M. Dubois, *12 Etudes variees* (Leduc); H. Glantz, *The Complete Harry Glantz* (C. Colin); E. Sachse, *100 Etudes* (International).

Solos: E. Bozza, *Badinage* (Leduc); W. Hartley, *Sonatina* (Accura Music); Webber, *Suite in F Major* (Mills).

Technique: Scales as in level 5 with increased speeds, plus quintuplet grouping. Arpeggios as in level 5, plus augmented, dominant seventh and diminished seventh.

Level 7

A study of the more advanced material with emphasis on recital literature. Addition of G and E transpositions. Work with the C trumpet.

Typical Material:

Studies: Brandt/Nagel, *34 Studies* (International); G. Bartold, *Orchestral Excerpts Vol. I and II.* (International); M. Gisondi, *Bach for the Trumpet* (McGinnis and Marx); Nagel, *Speed Studies* (Mentor).

Solos: J. Haydn, *Concerto* (C. Fischer); E. Bozza, *Caprice* (Leduc); K. Riisager, *Concertino* (W. Hansen); F. Peeters, *Sonata* (Peters); H. Purcell, *Sonata in D Major* (R. King).

Technique: Same as level 6 with increased speeds.

Level 8

Further emphasis on transposition and solo repertoire. Continued study of the standard orchestral repertoire. Work with the D and piccolo B flat/A trumpets.

Typical Material:

Studies: R. Sabarich, *10 Etudes* (Selmer); G. Bartold, *Orchestral Excerpts, Vol. III, IV, and V* (International); M. Broiles, *Studies and Duets, Vol. II* (McGinnis and Marx).

Solos: J. N. Hummel, *Concerto* (R. King); P. Hindemith, *Sonata* (Schott); J. Casterede, *Sonatine* (Leduc); G. F. Handel, *Suite in D Major* (Musica Rara).

Technique: Same as level 8 with increased speeds.

Level 9

Continued emphasis on orchestral repertoire and recital pieces.

Typical Material:

Studies: M. Broiles, *Studies and Duets, Vol I* (McGinnis and Marx); R. Voisin, *Orchestral Excerpts* (International); V. Brandt, *24 Last Studies* (International).

Solos: K. Kennan, *Sonata* (Music Publishers Holding); Bitsch, *4 Variations on a Theme by Scarlatti* (Leduc); A. Arutunian, *Concerto* (International); J. M. Molter, *Concerto No. 1* (Brass Press).

Technique: Same as level 8 with increased speeds.

Level 10

A coverage of all types of styles and techniques used for solo, orchestral and ensemble playing. Memorization of standard orchestral excerpts and selected recital pieces.

Typical Material:

Studies: M. Bitsch, *20 Etudes* (Leduc); C. Chaynes, *15 Etudes* (Leduc); V. Reynolds, *48 Etudes* (G. Schirmer); Rossbach, *Strauss Orchestral Excerpts* (International); Hoehne, *Wagner Orchestral Excerpts, Vol. I and II* (International).

Solos: G. Enesco, *Legend* (International); L. Mozart, *Concerto* (Billaudot); C. Chaynes, *Concerto* (Leduc); G. P. Telemann, *Concerto in D Major* (N. Simrock).

Technique: Same as level 9 with increased speeds.

Chapter 29
Trumpet Ensembles

Homogenous trumpet ensembles can be valuable to both trumpet students and teachers. Some people might see only the recreational value in these, and while this in itself is valid, their actual merit goes much deeper. Trumpet ensembles may include any number of players and the literature varies in difficulty from easy to advanced. This makes the implementation of trumpet ensembles applicable to class lessons and sectional rehearsals. Directors may choose from a wealth of the duet repertoire with one or more players on a part, or from selections with as many as 12 individual parts. When using only one person per part, students are faced with demands which they are unlikely to have the opportunity to experience in a large concert band. On the other hand, having more than one player per part will make them aware of unison intonation exactness and uniform concepts of tone, dynamics and articulation. In some high school music programs with excellent bands the director works with students most of the time in sectional rehearsals. The complete band may rehearse together only once or twice a week. While this may be far from ideal in the opinion of many directors, it is possible to teach effectively with this arrangement. Knowledge of the trumpet ensemble repertoire, or repertoire for any homogenous section, gives the director the opportunity to provide quality material for study to supplement the band literature. It may also be used to provide a contrast in the periods and styles of the music the entire band may be performing.

A variety of timbres can be achieved within the ensemble by using a mixture of cornets, trumpets and flugelhorns. For players at the college level, additional timbres may be created by using C, D, E flat and even piccolo trumpets, although these combinations usually present intonation problems which require a thorough knowledge of the instruments and the problems unique to each of them. Some people might rationalize combining mezzo-soprano and bass trumpets together to perform the brass quartet repertoire, but I feel this is stretching the homogenous point a bit too far.

James Ode and Herbert C. Mueller, trumpeters in the Ithaca Brass Quintet and faculty members at Ithaca College, compiled annotated lists of material for two trumpets. Dr. Ode's list includes trumpet duet collections while Mr. Mueller's represents two-trumpet literature with accompaniments. These lists were part of a presentation at the 1976 National Trumpet Symposium in Norman, Oklahoma and are both published in the *International Trumpet Guild Journal, Volume 1,* October 1976.

The list below, while not attempting to present all works available for trumpet ensembles, should provide a point of departure for groups of various sizes and levels of advancement who wish to investigate this literature.

E—Easy   M—Medium   D—Difficult

Two Trumpets
Casterede, J. *Six Pieces Breves en Duo*—LeDuc (D)
Corrette, M. *Two Divertimenti*—International (D)
Stravinsky, I. *Fanfare for a New Theatre*—Boosey and Hawkes (D)

Two Trumpet Collections
Biber, H. *12 Trumpet Duets*—The Brass Press (M)
Gates, E. *Odd Meter Duets*—Sam Fox (ME)
Hering, S. *Miniature Classics for Two Trumpets*—Carl Fischer (E)
Hering, S. *Trumpets for Two*—Carl Fischer (E)
Mazas *Interesting Duets*—David Gornston (M)
Neibig, A. *26 Duets*—International (M)
Nelson, B. *Advanced Duets*—Charles Colin (D)
Voxman, H. *Selected Duets* (2 volumes)—Rubank (ME–D)
Wehner, W. *20 Modern Duets*—Lucien Caillet (D)

Three Trumpets
Anderson, L. *Bugler's Holiday*—Mills (M)
Donato, A. *Sonatina for 3 B flat trumpets*—G. Schirmer (MD)
Elwell, H. *Fanfares Strictly for Trumpets*—Charles Colin (M)
Phillips, B. *Trio for Trumpets*—King (MD)

Four Trumpets
Dubensky *Suite for Four Trumpets*—Charles Colin (MD)
Gillis, D. *Sonatina*—Boosey and Hawkes (MD)
Scheidt, S. *Canzona*—King (MD)
Sherman, R., ed. *Three Early Madrigals*—Ensemble (ME)

Five Trumpets
LoPresti, R. *Suite for Five Trimpets*—Shawnee (MD)
Reynolds, V. *Music for 5 Trumpets*—King (D)

Seven Trumpets
Altenberg, J. E. *Concerto for clarini and timpani*—King (D)

Chapter 30
Instruments of Historical Interest

It is becoming increasingly apparent that trumpet players of today need to be versatile individuals. Those holding positions in symphony orchestras are expected to perform a wide variety of literature on trumpets in several keys. Trumpet teachers at the college level are expected to excel in teaching, play solo recitals, know and perform the chamber music repertoire, and often have expertise in a secondary field such as theory, history, or composition.

A new dimension has been added to these demands with the revival of the performance of early music on reproductions of instruments from the respective historical periods. In recent years a variety of collegia and Renaissance societies have begun to appear in cities and on university campuses. Playing in these ensembles has provided the trumpeter with another outlet for creative musical activity or employability. The purpose of this chapter is to give a brief overview of three of the most common instruments used in this capacity at the present time. Tremendous historical research has been done on each of these instruments and detailed books and articles are available for those interested in further investigation. My intent is to introduce these instruments to readers who otherwise might not be aware of their existence and perhaps kindle some interest in further investigating performance possibilities on them.

The Cornetto

Many people have the mistaken idea that because of the similarity in name, the *cornetto* has a close relationship to the modern cornet. The *cornetto* actually represents a combination of the cup-shaped mouthpiece of the brasses and the basic construction and fingering of recorders. The instrument was used extensively during the Renaissance and into the Early Baroque. It was probably the most versatile instrument of that period, having a unique range of tone qualities from the sound of a soft voice to the brilliance of a trumpet. It could be used as a solo voice in dance music, as a reinforcement for an internal voice part in a choral work, or even to play a continuo line.

In Germany the *cornetto* was called a *zink*. There were several varieties and sizes of the *cornetto* as was the case with many instruments during that period. The family consisted of the *cornettino*, the curved *cornetto*,

a straight *cornetto* (*cornetto diritto*) similar to the curved *cornetto*; a straight *cornetto muto*, which again was similar but had the mouthpiece carved into the instrument rather than detachable; and the *tenor cornetto* (*cornetto torto*), also called a *lysarden*, which was S shaped. There are a few references to a *bass cornetto* but this instrument was quite rare. The tone quality and unwieldly size of the tenor and bass instruments made them less acceptable and the *sackbut* or the *serpent* were often substituted. The *cornettino* and curved *cornetto* are the instruments most frequently used today.

Cornetto Ranges

Cornettino

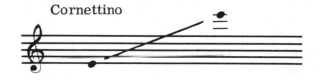

Cornetto

Tenor Cornetto (Lysarden)

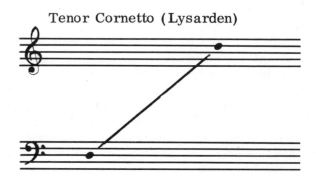

The curved instruments were made of wood in two halves with the bore gouged out smoothly. The halves were then glued together and the outside was carved into an octagonal shape. The *cornetto* was covered with leather to prevent it from cracking or separating and to facilitate holding. The *cornetto* has six finger holes

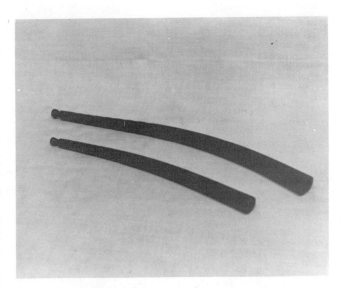

Fig. 76 Cornetto (top) and Cornettino (bottom)

and a thumb hole. (Some French instruments had seven finger holes and no thumb hole.)

Modern reproductions of the instrument are made essentially the same way although there is a less expensive reproduction available made of molded resin.

Mouthpieces for the *cornetto* were sometimes made of ivory or horn. Modern adaptations are generally of wood, metal or plastic. The most common mouthpiece was acorn shaped with a thin rim and shallow cup. Some players choose to play on this same shape mouthpiece; however, there is a tendency for the sound to be restricted if the lip swells up into this shallow cup. For that reason, many of today's players choose to use a wider, deeper cup with somewhat larger rim—more of a compromise with today's trumpet mouthpiece.

There is a wide variety of mouthpiece placement possibilities, as confirmed by many engravings by artists of the Renaissance. Many trumpeters prefer to play in the center of the lips with the same vibrating surface as used with their normal embouchure. There is considerable evidence that many of the performers of that period played on the side of the mouth. The thinner lips at the corners of the mouth are thought to have been more successful in producing a tone on the small mouthpiece. This also enabled the performer, who customarily doubled on several instruments, to use the center portion of the lips for reed placement when playing the woodwind instruments. Regardless of the embouchure used, the development of sensitivity, control and aural perception are important on the *cornetto*, as the tone can be very unsteady and it is often necessary to correct faulty intonation with lip adjustments.

Fig. 77 Cornetto Playing Position

The left-hand position over the tone holes is similar to that used with the recorder, but the right hand is quite different and often presents the greatest problems for cornetto players. The performer must to be able to support the instrument with the right hand alone

Fig. 78 Cornetto—Right Hand Position

with no tone holes covered. The right hand position
to accomplish this uses the side of the index finger,
the thumb and the tip of the little finger. The index
finger must be kept in a position so that it can support
the instrument and still cover the fourth tone hole.
This can become quite uncomfortable when playing
for long periods.

For this reason some players install a thumb rest
so the right-hand position becomes more like that used
with a clarinet.

The *cornetto* entered a decline with the advent of
the natural trumpet, with its ability to play the stirring
clarino parts, and the Baroque oboe, which was easier
to play in tune.

Beginning literature for the *cornetto* may be adapted
from many easy recorder or flute method books. An
interesting book devoted exclusively to elementary
cornetto playing is Volker Kernbach's *How to Play
the Treble Cornett*. Two articles which also are quite
informative are, "First Steps Toward Playing the Cornett," by Christopher Monk from *Early Music*, Vol.
3, Nos. 2 and 3, April and July 1975, and "A Handbook
for the Cornetto," by Ralph Dudgeon from the *Journal
of the International Trumpet Guild*, Vol. 3, No. 1.

Fig. 79 Natural Trumpet

The Natural Trumpet

The era of the natural trumpet has to be one of
the most exciting periods in music history for trumpet
enthusiasts. This period was the time when the trumpet
was recognized as a virtuoso instrument and the artists
of the day were looked upon with great esteem. The
natural trumpet was twice the length of our modern
instruments of comparable key and the performer was
called upon to play in the high harmonic range of the
instrument in order to produce notes that were only
one scale step apart. Notes which were out of tune
could be adjusted to some degree with the embouchure.
Holes were added to some instruments around the
middle of the 18th Century. One to three holes were
placed at critical nodes. When the holes were vented
(opened), the pitch could be corrected to a point where
it was much more acceptable. A valuable book which
deals extensively with the natural trumpet is *The Music
and History of the Baroque Trumpet before 1721,* by
Don L. Smithers. Other selected sources of historical
information are included in the annotated bibliography
in Chapter 32.

Modern use of the natural trumpet is usually as a
solo instrument with organ or as an obbligato line with
vocal solos. As with the other historical instruments
in this chapter, examination of the natural trumpet helps

us understand and appreciate the modern instrument
while at the same time keeping us aware of its heritage.

The Keyed Trumpet

The keyed trumpet was developed because of a need
for chromaticism which was not attainable on the natural
trumpet. The existence of this instrument was relatively
short. There is controversy as to when the instrument
actually was invented. Some research indicates it was
invented by the prominent trumpeter, Anton Weidinger,
in 1801. In recent years this has been disputed since
Haydn's *Concerto in E flat,* written in 1796 for "Clarino
Solo," had to employ an instrument which had more
notes than those performed by clarino players—in the
literal sense. It now appears that such an instrument
may have existed as early as 1770. The instrument used
in the Haydn *Concerto* had five keys. Others of the
period had anywhere from four to six keys. The instrument was held horizontally with the keys covering tone
holes. When the keys were opened, one at a time,
the pitch was raised by half steps. The key nearest
the bell was opened first and the sequence continued
progressively along the instrument. The tone quality
varied as each key was opened; consequently, the
maximum number of keys open yielded the poorest
tone. The first keyed trumpets developed were pitched
in D or E flat. Early in the 19th century instruments

were constructed in G, A or A flat and had crooks which could be added for the lower pitches.

Present-day interest in keyed trumpets is for the most part limited to performance of the Haydn and Hummel *Concertos*. As the public is accustomed to hearing these works performed on a modern valve trumpet, it cannot help but be disturbed when hearing the lack of uniformity of tone between notes on the keyed instrument. In spite of this limitation, having the opportunity to hear the keyed trumpet played furnishes valuable insight into the evolution of the present-day instrument.

Fig. 80 Keyed Trumpet (*Courtesy of Tromba Publications*.)

The keyed trumpet should not be confused with the keyed bugle which was developed later (c. 1810). The keyed bugle was popular in military bands and as a solo instrument. It was much more conical in shape and some had as many as 12 keys. Most were pitched in B flat or C. Through the efforts of the virtuoso soloist of the era, Ned Kendall, the instrument remained popular until the middle of the 19th Century.

Sources for Historical Instrument Reproductions

The Brass Press
159-8th Ave.
Nashville, TN 37203

Gunter Korber
Filandastrasse 29
1 Berlin 41
West Germany

Historical Wind Reproductions
P.O. Box 141
Redlands, CA 92373

Kelischek Workshops
Brasstown
North Carolina 28902

Meinl and Lauber Historical Brass Instruments
8192 Geretsried
Postfach 1342
West Germany

Janet Miller
307 Rich's Dugway Rd.
Rochester, NY 14625

Moeck Verlag und Musikinstrumentwerk
D-31 Celle
Postfach 143
West Germany

C. W. Monk
Stock Farm House
Churt Farnham Survey
Hindhead 991
Great Britain

Pipe and Tabor
929 Danby Rd.
Ithaca, NY 14850

Tromba Publications
1859 York Street
Denver, Colorado 80206

Rainer Weber
8301 Bayerback Landsheet
West Germany

Chapter 31
The International Trumpet Guild

Trumpet players throughout the world are bonded together professionally by an organization known as the International Trumpet Guild. The Guild was formed in 1974 and its first annual meeting was held in Bloomington, Indiana in May 1975.

The purposes as stated by the organization are to promote communication among trumpet players around the world and to improve the artistic level of performance, teaching, and literature associated with the trumpet. In pursuit of these goals, the ITG sponsors annual meetings which include clinics, recitals, lectures on acoustics, physiology, history and other subjects related to the instrument. The annual meetings also include solo and orchestral audition contests for students and provide professional adjudication sessions for students wishing to be evaluated.

Activities not necessarily connected with the annual meetings include presentation of student scholarships, sponsorship of composition contests for the trumpet as a solo and ensemble instrument, presentation of honors to those who have given distinguished service to the instrument, and establishment of a close working relationship with music teachers.

There are five classes of membership—professional, student, associate, honorary, and patron. Many of the leading trumpet performers and teachers of this country and the world are members.

In addition to the parent organization, there are numerous state and local chapters which sponsor regularly scheduled activities on a regional level. Many of these chapters bring in recitalists and clinicians, give scholarships and offer a myriad of activities at the local level.

The major publication of the organization is the *Journal of the International Trumpet Guild* which is published each fall. There is also the *ITG Newsletter,* published three times yearly. These two publications are the primary source for the seriously interested trumpeter to keep abreast of new publications, technology, research, programs, recordings and other aspects of what is current in the world of trumpet performance and teaching.

Major officers of the ITG rotate every two years, so it would be impossible to give current persons in these positions. Persons wishing to affiliate with The International Trumpet Guild will find appropriate officers listed in the annual directory of *Musical America* magazine.

Chapter 32
Annotated Bibliography

TEXTBOOKS

Trumpet Texts:

Bush, Irving R. *Artistic Trumpet Technique and Study.* Hollywood, California: Highland Music Company, 1962.

An excellent study of trumpet teaching and performance. The author is a member of the trumpet section of the Los Angeles Philharmonic and designs and manufactures trumpet mouthpieces. Statements are clear and easily understood. Students as young as high school age would find this interesting and informative.

Cardosa, Wilfredo. *High Trumpets, Vol. I–II.* Buenos Aires, Argentina: The Author, 1969.

This book represents the first two volumes of a 24 volume encyclopedia on the trumpet. Volumes I and II deal with technical problems of the high instruments, from the D trumpet through the three and four valve piccolo trumpets.

Dale, Delbert. *Trumpet Technique.* London. Oxford University Press, 1967.

A small, but detailed book which gives an overview of many aspects of trumpet performance and teaching.

Davidson, Louis. *Trumpet Technique.* Rochester, New York: Wind Music Incorporated. 1970.

The text discusses various important fundamentals. Approximately two-thirds of the book is devoted to examples of various routines and drills.

Grocock, Robert. *Advanced Method for Trumpet.* Greencastle, Ind. The Argee Music Press, 1968.

Divided into two major parts. Part I includes text and examples on all aspects of trumpet playing. Some are quite detailed, others are brief. The longer chapters are on ornamentation, principles of musical performance (illustrated by many passages from trumpet literature), transposition, and constructive practice. Part II includes scale and arpeggio exercises and tonguing studies which relate to the text in Part I.

Lowrey, Alvin L. *Trumpet Discography.* Denver, Colorado: The National Trumpet Symposium, n.d.

A collection of three volumes. The first deals exclusively with the many recordings of Maurice André; the second, a compilation of individual trumpet performers; and the third, homogeneous and heterogeneous brass ensembles. The volumes are cross-indexed by performer, composer, ensemble name, and in some cases historical period. This book should be in all school libraries and in the collections of trumpet audiophiles.

General Brass Texts:

Bate, Philip. *The Trumpet and Trombone: An Outline of their History, Development and Construction.* New York: W. W. Norton and Co., Inc., 1966.

A detailed, scholarly approach to the trumpet and trombone. This book includes many illustrations, including cut-away drawings of valves. The book should be in every brass teacher's reference library.

Brass Anthology. Evanston, Illinois: The Instrumentalist, 1969.

A collection of articles from *The Instrumentalist* magazine from 1946–1968. Many are written by some of the major names in brass performance and teaching.

Farkas, Philip. *The Art of Brass Playing.* Bloomington, Indiana: Brass Publications, 1962.

A treatise dealing with the embouchure on the various brass instruments. It includes muscle function, mouthpiece placement, lip aperture, articulation, mouthpiece pressure and breathing. Comprehensive and detailed.

Fox, Fred. *Essentials of Brass Playing.* Los Angeles: The Author, 1974.

The book is thorough but does not become burdened with details. The author looks for alternatives to the "brute-force" approach to brass playing. Stresses intelligent application of embouchure and air-column support.

King, Robert. *Brass Players' Guide.* North Easton, Mass.: Robert King Music Company, 1978.

The catalog of music for brass instruments from various publishers marketed by the Robert King Music Company. Includes a complete listing of all presently available solos, etudes, orchestral excerpts, texts, chamber music and brass ensembles. Revised yearly. Publishers list included.

Rasmussen, Mary. *A Teacher's Guide to the Literature of Brass Instruments.* Durham, New Hampshire: Brass Quarterly, 1964. 2nd Edition published by Appleyard Publications, Box 111, Durham, New Hampshire, 1968.

An essential book in any teacher's library. Contains lists of solos, etudes, ensembles, and textbooks. Materials are graded for level of difficulty with notation of special performance problems.

Weast, Robert. *Brass Performance: An Analytical Text of the Physical Processes, Problems and Technique of Brass.* New York: McGinnis and Marx, 1961.

A comprehensive book with some unique features, including a stroboscopic study of brass players' lips inside a transparent mouthpiece. It allows the examination of the vibration of both the top and bottom lip.

Brass Class Methods:

Mueller, Herbert. *Learning to Teach Through Playing: A Brass Method.* Reading, Massachusetts: Addison-Wesley Publishing Company, 1968.

A balanced text of theory and practice for the heterogeneous brass class. Includes lists of recordings, dissertations, catalogs and books for supplementary study.

Zorn, Jay D. *Brass Ensemble Method for Music Educators.* Belmont, California: Wadsworth Publishing Company, Inc. 1977.

A good balance of teaching and performance material. Classes could supplement the book with additional readings from specific pedagogical books for each instrument.

Historical Texts:

Altenburg, Johann Ernst. *Trumpeters' and Kettledrummers' Art.* Nashville, Tenn.: The Brass Press, 1974.

Translated by Edward H. Tarr, this book gives a complete background on Baroque trumpet performance and teaching. It gives insights into life styles and social status of trumpeters in the 18th Century. Many of the ideas included are applicable to performers playing clarino parts on modern instruments or enthusiasts who are learning to play historical reproductions.

Barbour, J. Murray. *Trumpets, Horns and Music.* East Lansing, Michigan: Michigan State University Press, 1964.

Traces the use of the trumpet and the horn from 1600–1830. Musical examples illustrate the trumpet's use in rhythm, melody, harmony and in modulations. The book is an interesting study on the development of more advanced demands on trumpet performers by composers of that era.

Bendinelli, Cesare. *The Entire Art of Trumpet Playing, 1614.* English translation and Critical commentary by Edward H. Tarr. Nashville, Tenn.: The Brass Press, 1975.

The earliest trumpet method now known (preceding Girolamo Fantini's *Modo per imparare a sonare di tromba* by 24 years).
The book gives insight into the techniques of trumpet playing around 1600. There is discussion of protruding the chin, the use of syllables, tonguing, the motif *dran* (a technique of lightly touching a note and quickly passing to a second note with a slight accent) and methods of trumpet ensemble playing.

Dahlquist, Reine. *The Keyed Trumpet and Its Greatest Virtuoso, Anton Weidinger.* Nashville, Tenn.: The Brass Press, 1975.

An excellent study on the instrument used in the original performances of the Haydn and Hummel concertos. Discusses the keyed trumpet's influence at that time and relates it to similar instruments of that period.

Eliason, Robert E. *Keyed Bugles in the United States.* Washington, D.C.: Smithsonian Institution Press, 1972.

This booklet traces the history and development of the keyed bugle from its patent in 1910. Excellent photographs of instruments by various manufacturers.

Robinson, Trevor. *The Amateur Wind Instrument Maker.* Amherst, Mass.: University of Massachusetts Press, 1973.

An interesting book for the do-it-yourself enthusiast. Among the instruments described are the cornetto, natural trumpet and hunting horn. Included are sources for tools, wood and other materials. The book also includes a list of some museums with instrument collections.

Smithers, Don L. *The Music and History of the Baroque Trumpet before 1721.* Syracuse, N.Y.: Syracuse University Press, 1973.

A detailed study of all aspects concerning the trumpet during the period from 1600–1721. Dr. Smithers, highly respected as a musician and musicologist, has provided a valuable source for all those interested in this significant historical period.

Other Related Texts:

Benade, Arthur H. *Fundamentals of Musical Acoustics.* London: Oxford University Press, 1976.

This detailed book will be valuable to all musicians. Among other things, it includes an interesting study on the compatibility of the trumpet mouthpiece to the instrument.

Benade, Arthur H. *Horns, Strings, and Harmony.* Garden City, N.Y.: Doubleday and Company, Inc., 1960.

From the Science Study Series books by distinguished authors. A study of the physics of sound, designed for comprehension by laymen and young students.

Carnovale, Norbert. *Twentieth-Century Music for Trumpet and Orchestra.* Nashville, Tenn.: The Brass Press, 1975.

An annotated list of graded trumpet solos which includes a listing of some special technical problems.

Farkas, Philip. *The Art of Musicianship.* Bloomington, Indiana: Musical Publications, 1976.

This experienced performer and teacher has compiled a treatise on the skills, knowledge and sensitivity needed by the mature musician to perform in an artistic and professional manner. Should be required reading for all music students.

Farr, Linda Anne. *A Trumpeter's Guide to Orchestral Excerpts.* Nashville, Tenn.: The Brass Press, 1977.

A composer index to over 1000 excerpts contained in fifty-nine volumes of orchestral trumpet literature. This book will be indispensible to the student who aspires to a career as an orchestral musician.

Solos

Arutunian, Alexander, *Concerto.* International, 1967.

This major work by the contemporary Russian composer is becoming one of the best known trumpet concertos. Romantic and sometimes very brilliant, it is within the playing capabilities of mature high school students. Level 9.

Baines, Francis. *Pastorale.* Schott, 1952.

A flowing, melodic solo. An excellent study piece for breath control and phrasing. Level 4.

Bartles, Alfred H. *Sonatina.* The Brass Press, 1971.

This solo for unaccompanied trumpet is in a conservative style in respect to melodic material and technical demands. It would make a good choice for a student's first attempt with unaccompanied literature. Level 5.

Castérède, Jacques. *Sonatine for C Trumpet and Piano.* Alphonse Leduc, 1956.

An interesting three movement work from the contemporary French literature. Level 8.

Chance, John Barnes. *Credo.* Boosey and Hawkes, 1964.

An intense solo with piano accompaniment utilizing double tonguing and uncommon meters. Level 5.

Fiocco, Joseph. Don Owen (ed.). *Arioso.* Presser, 1973.

A solo with phrasing and control demands for the young player. Level 3.

Goedicke, Alexander. *Concert Etude, Op. 49.* Leeds, 1946.

A brilliant solo that typifies what we have come to expect from many of the Russian composers of this century. Double tonguing is used extensively. Level 5.

Hartley, Walter. *Sonatina.* Accura Music, 1956.

A conservative, but interesting, three movement work by this recognized American composer. The work has a moderately difficult solo part, but coordination with the piano accompaniment is relatively easy. Orchestra accompaniment available. Level 6.

Haydn, Franz Joseph. Goeyens (ed.). *Trumpet Concerto.* Carl Fischer, n.d.

Probably the most widely known trumpet concerto. There are six editions of this solo available at the present time with only minor differences in articulation patterns and dynamics. Students should be encouraged to study several of the different cadenza possibilities. Level 7.

Hindemith, Paul. *Sonate.* B. Schott's Soehne, 1939.

One of the monumental pieces of trumpet repertoire. For the music student with mature musical concepts. Difficult piano accompaniment. Level 8.

Hovhaness, Alan. *Prayer of St. Gregory.* Peer, 1952.

A short, but interesting solo in the melismatic style usually associated with this composer. Accompaniment may be organ or string ensemble. Level 3.

Hummel, Johann Nepomuk. Armando Ghitalla (ed.). *Concerto for Trumpet.* Robert King, 1959.

At present there are no fewer than nine editions of this work. The Ghitalla edition in E flat major is reasonable for most study and recital purposes. It also has a band accompaniment available. The Tarr edition is in the original key of E major. Level 8.

Kennan, Kent. *Sonata for Trumpet and Piano.* Warner Bros., 1956.

One of the major works from the trumpet solo repertoire. This three movement work should be studied by all serious trumpet students. Level 9.

Molter, Johann M. Stephen L. Glover and John F. Sawyer (editors). *Concerto No. 2.* The Brass Press, 1971.

One of the most beautiful of the Baroque Trumpet concertos. The solo presents significant problems in *tessitura* and should be reserved for the most advanced students. Level 10.

Purcell, Henry. Armando Ghitalla (ed.). *Sonata.* Robert King, 1960.

An excellent solo for the D or piccolo A trumpet. It is very much idiomatic of the period and makes a good study piece as well as recital solo. Organ accompaniment. Level 7.

Purcell, Henry. Wesley Ramsay (ed.). "Trumpet Aria" from *The Indian Queen.* The Brass Press, 1975.

A work for high school or early college students. Includes an effective organ accompaniment. Level 4.

Reed, Alfred. *Ode for Trumpet.* Charles H. Hansen, 1956.

A tuneful ballad which is an attractive solo piece for the high school student. Band accompaniment available. Level 4.

Sanders, Robert. *Square Dance.* Galaxy, 1959.

A lively piece for the high school student. Fairly easy to put together with the piano accompaniment. Level 4.

Shapero, Harold. *Sonata for C Trumpet and Piano.* Southern, 1956.

A two movement work which is exceedingly challenging to both the soloist and accompanist. The first movement has a blues influence and the second is in sonata form. Level 9.

Stevens, Halsey. *Sonata for Trumpet and Piano.* C. F. Peters Co., 1959.

A very demanding work for both the soloist and accompanist. Intricate rhythmic figurations make this work difficult both individually and collectively. This piece should be in every serious trumpeter's repertoire. Level 8.

Viviani, Giovanni. Edward Tarr, (ed.) *Two Sonatas for Trumpet.* Musica Rara, 1969.

These two sonatas from the late seventeenth century utilize flowing lines in the solo trumpet over a chromatic bass line. The *Sonata Seconda* is particularly good as an introductory solo for the piccolo trumpet. Level 6–8.

Webber, Lloyd. *Suite in F Major.* Mills, 1958.

An interesting four movement work for the high school or college student. Most students will enjoy the tuneful melodies. Level 5.

Wolff, S. Drummond (arr.). *Baroque Composers of the "Chapels Royal."* Concordia, 1969.

A collection of Baroque organ works with optional trumpets and timpani. These pieces are suitable for ceremonial occasions in churches. Some of the selections are ideal for introducing a student to D trumpet performance. Level 4–7.

Wolff, S. Drummond (ed. and arr.). *Suite for Organ from the French Baroque.* Concordia, 1973.

A collection of organ music with one or two trumpets and optional tympani. Although the piece is called a "Suite," the movements can be effectively used as individual pieces. Both B flat and C trumpet parts are included. Level 4–7.

Etudes

Arban, J.J.B.L. Goldman and Smith (ed.). *Complete Conservatory Method.* Carl Fischer, n.d.

There are several editions of the Arban book available with varying amounts of material in each. The most complete edition is by Maire, but the price of the three volume set makes it prohibitive for many students. Level 2–7.

Blatter, Alfred and Paul Zonn. Annotated and Edited by David Hickman. *Contemporary Trumpet Studies.* Denver, Colorado: Tromba Publications, 1976.

This book is divided into six sections. The first is a notational guide. The remaining five are studies and duets in the following categories: Metric Studies; Rythmic Studies; Intervalic Studies; Twentieth-Century Studies; and Aleatoric Studies. A great help in the preparation and performance of contemporary music. Level 8–10.

Broiles, Mel. *Trumpet Studies and Duets, Vol. I.* McGinnis and Marx, 1958.

The first of three volumes by this outstanding trumpeter. The etudes are quite difficult, but tonal. The duets are very challenging. The second and third volumes are similar in format. Level 6–9.

Chaynes, Charles. *15 Etudes for Trumpet.* Alphonse Leduc, 1959.

An excellent collection of really difficult studies. Awkward intervals and fingering patterns. Musically of high quality and very challenging. Level 10.

Concone, Giuseppe. Transcribed by John F. Sawyer. *Lyrical Studies for Trumpet.* The Brass Press, 1972.

An essential book for developing musical phrasing with young students. Level 3.

Dubois, Pierre Max. *Douze Etudes Variees.* Alphonse Leduc, 1959.

These 12 etudes present a nice mixture of melodic, rhythmic, and technical problems. They prepare students for studying the contemporary French trumpet literature. Level 9.

Gates, Everett. *Odd Meter Etudes.* Gornston, 1962.

A collection of 21 etudes to acquaint students with unusual meters. Not overly difficult technically, but when combined with the rhythmic and musical judgments necessary, they can be very challenging for high school and college students. Level 5.

Gisondi, Michael J. *Bach for the Trumpet or Cornet.* McGinnis and Marx, 1956.

A collection of some of the well-known themes from the various works of Bach. Interesting and challenging for study purposes. Level 3–7.

Hering, Sigmund. *The Orchestra Trumpeter.* Carl Fischer, Inc. 1970.

Intended as an introductory book for trumpet transposition. The melodies are tuneful. Several keys are introduced. Level 3.

Hering, Sigmund. *Thirty Two Etudes.* Carl Fischer, Inc. 1972.

The original edition of this book was printed in 1943, but the exercises are still very useful for the beginning-intermediate student. This also may be used as beginning transposition studies. Level 2.

Hickman, David. *The Piccolo Trumpet: Duets, Etudes, Orchestral Excerpts.* Denver, Colorado: Tromba Publications, 1973.

A practical book for introduction to the piccolo trumpet. Exercises to aid adaptation to the instrument with transition through etudes and into some of the better known orchestral literature using piccolo trumpet. Level 7–10.

Kinyon, John. *Breeze-Easy Method for Trumpet.* (2 volumes) Witmark, 1958, 1959.

A good beginning book for private or homogeneous class instruction. Easy to read and suitable for range, technical, and tone development of beginning students. Level 1 and 2.

Nagel, Robert. *Speed Studies for Trumpet.* Sam Fox, 1965.

This book is a logical sequential step for the student who has developed his technique with Herbert L. Clarke's *Technical Studies.* It contains many difficult fingering patterns and are excellent for technical control and reading. Level 5–7.

Nagel, Robert. *Trumpet Studies in Contemporary Music.* Edward B. Marks, 1975.

A collection of 14 etudes in a variety of contemporary styles. A good choice as an introductory book to this type of material. Level 5–7.

Reynolds, Verne. *48 Etudes for Trumpet.* Schirmer, 1971.

An adaptation for trumpet of Reynolds' etudes for French horn. They are challenging technically and they make use of the total range of the instrument. Level 9.

Stevens, Thomas. *Contemporary Trumpet Studies.* Billandot, 1976.

An outstanding collection of studies dealing with the performance of contemporary literature. Most etudes have explanations regarding performance difficulties and notation interpretation. Level 8–10.